The
BROWN BAG
COOKBOOK

35

Jodi
   mayonnaise
   ¾ m. to ¼ c. yogurt
   cuts down fat

121 tuna egg boats
131 Slenderella's Stix
121 ~ Drumsticks
123 Meal In a Bar
164 Power- Packed Cookies
              No-Bake

Library of Congress Cataloging in Publication Data
Sloan, Sara.
  The brown bag cookbook.

  1. Lunchbox cookery. I. Title.
TX735.S63 1984 641.5′3 83-27335
ISBN 0-913589-01-2

Cover and interior design: Trezzo-Braren Studio
Decorative illustrations: Loretta Trezzo
Printing: Capital City Press

Williamson Publishing
Charlotte, Vermont 05445

Manufactured in the United States of America

Fifth Printing February 1987

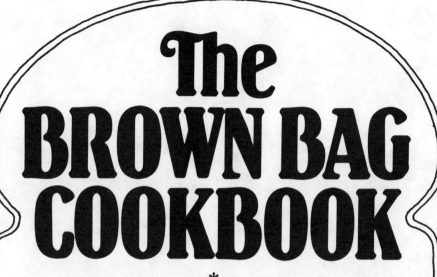

The BROWN BAG COOKBOOK

*

NUTRITIOUS PORTABLE LUNCHES FOR KIDS AND GROWN~UPS

by Sara Sloan

ILLUSTRATED BY LORETTA TREZZO

WILLIAMSON PUBLISHING CO.

CHARLOTTE, VERMONT 05445

ACKNOWLEDGEMENTS

To those kids and teachers who strolled into school cafeterias carrying their lunches in brown paper bags – and aroused my curiosity as to the contents.

To Claudine Whitley for her inspiration and encouragement and those endless hours at the typewriter.

To Judi whose mom insisted she buy school lunches.

To Bob Bennett for making this book happen.

To Susan Williamson for her editorial work.

CONTENTS

Dedicated
to
My Favorite Totables:
Julia Claire and Joanna Rose

INTRODUCTION

Why is a food service director with 31 years of experience in the public schools writing a book about brown bag lunches? I confess that on numerous occasions I, too, have been a brown bagger, especially when those "mystery meals" were served at school.

However, any self-respecting food service director cringes at the sight of all those colorful lunch boxes and brown bags being toted into the school cafeteria by students and teachers. Hopefully, though, food service directors, teachers, parents, and increasing numbers of students, too, share the same lunchtime objectives – providing nutritious, varied, appealing lunches that will be eaten rather than tossed away.

And brown baggers are not just to be found in schools. Portable lunches are eaten everywhere – in factories and offices, on high-rise girders at construction sites, at roadside tables, in treehouses, on bicycles and boats – even in executive board rooms.

JOIN THE BROWN BAG REBELLION

The secret is out, and brown baggers abound for a myriad of good reasons. The common denominator seems to be more control – more control over nutrition, over time, over expense, over food choices and preparation, and over environment. One thing is for sure, portable lunches are fashionable, whether you do business over veal cordon bleu, a burger, or a PB and J.

Nowadays, office workers can find respite during the workday with a lunchtime break outdoors for eating, sunning, and people watching. Some people arrange a portable feast complete with a colorful gingham cloth, a good book or radio, and plenty of fresh air. Some packers prefer dining in a group, each person contributing his or her favorite spreadable. Many employees pack lunches because their companies provide comfortable in-house eating facilities, including well-kept dining areas with portable ovens, toasters, and, even, refrigerators.

The increased awareness in fitness and good nutrition plays an important part in the on-going brown bag rebellion. People realize they simply can't depend on many cafeterias and fast-food outlets to offer nutritionally sound, carefully prepared lunches. People of all ages are unwilling to accept overcooked, vitamin-depleted vegetables, overbreaded deep-fried meats and fish, and oversweetened syrupy fruits. They've found their own alternatives.

Then there are those who skip lunch to make time for a trip to the bank, laundry, or gas station and settle for a "meal-in-a-bar" which is inexpensive, and easy to eat, but does not provide the satisfaction of a real meal. Even the protein in this on-the-go meal is usually wrapped in carbohydrate sources that are digested quickly, thus staving off hunger for only a short time. If you have to settle for such a meal once in a while, at least choose a bar balanced with healthy protein, fat, and carbohydrates. Try Sara's Nutritional Meal In a Bar (page 123).

Those who enjoy exercise or feel a need to shed a few pounds, can firm up and practice weight control by choosing their own trim-a-pound lunches that not only pack high nutrition, but also allow time for exercise. You can shed ten pounds a year by briskly walking an additional mile at lunchtime.

BROWN BAGGERS SAVE MONEY

Mr. David Lyon, a successful marketing specialist, prefers to have lunch at the Brown Bag Institute—his home. Mr. Lyon recently surveyed 60 million American brown baggers who pass up delicatessens, company cafeterias, and tax-deductible business lunches to keep greater control over what they eat and how much they eat. According to Mr. Lyon, baggers save an average of $1.80 a day.

Researchers have compared the costs of lunches prepared at home, a fancy restaurant, a take-out store, and a counter-type restaurant. Their findings were not surprising. For example, $.60 homemade chicken salad can cost as much as $6.75 in a tablecloth restaurant, $4.50 at a take-out store, or $3.95 in a counter-type restaurant. A roast beef sandwich costing $.90 cents at home costs up to $6.95 in a tablecloth restaurant, $3.00 as take-out, and $3.50 in a counter-type place. Instead of dropping at least $15 for five midday meals a week, the brown bagger packs a lunch and saves money.

Whatever the reason, everyone agrees that brown baggers enjoy eating what they like, where and when they like, and that there are plenty of easily prepared, fresh, nourishing culinary combinations possible.

SOME IMPORTANT PORTABLE LUNCH CONSIDERATIONS

For many individuals and families, dinner is the only meal that is planned with some attention given to nutrition, presentation, and flavor. It seems the most critical ingredient in breakfast is time or lack thereof; and for lunch, convenience plays an important role.

Yet, with a surprisingly small amount of fore-thought and time, lunch can be not only nutritious and good-tasting, it can also be just the emotional and physical pick-me-up needed to change a so-so day to a day with some sparkle.

What is needed can be as simple as tossing in some raisins and sunflower seeds with those old familiar carrot sticks, or pasting a sparkly sticker on a napkin as you tuck it in the bag. All of a sudden it's fun to open that brown bag again!

PLAN AHEAD!

The secret to packing nutritious lunches is planning and organization. Plan menus at least one week ahead, heeding family likes and dislikes, favorite recipes, and interesting combinations. Include totable "extras" in menu planning, and always keep in mind what foods you will have on hand from your dinner menus. It often works well to plan your dinners first, and then draw from those ingredients for your lunches.

If planning lunch menus seems like a lot of extra work, then do it gradually. Decide to plan one or two lunches per week for starters, or make a commitment to delete store-bought cookies and snack foods, substituting some of my not-too-sweet dessert ideas or some extras from the snack section. If you ease your way into planning and packing nutritious lunches, you'll find it takes little more time and effort than packing lunches as you do now—and the rewards are better health and well-being.

Once you have planned your menus, prepare a shopping list. The more organized you are, the less time you spend in the store; the less time you spend in the store, the less money you spend. Double-check your recipes against supplies on hand to avoid the frustrations of missing ingredients. Once your list is made, stick to it!

When planning portable lunches, be sure to consider:

Texture. Plan for both crunchy and smooth foods.

Flavor. Contrast strong flavors with mild ones, and remember that strong flavors often have strong odors, too. It's not too great to have your books or your team uniform smelling like dill pickles!

Color. Use colorful red, green, yellow, orange, and purple foods. Remember that visual appeal is important; if it doesn't look good, it won't whet anyone's appetite.

Temperature. Be sure you can keep hot foods hot and cold foods cold.

BE A WISE SHOPPER: ACQUIRE SUPERMARKET SAVVY

It takes strong willpower to walk through a supermarket and purchase only what's on your grocery list. Seventy percent of purchases made are unplanned, according to researchers, and the people who own supermarkets depend on this factor to make money. Impulse buying destroys your shape and your budget, too.

Be a calculating shopper. Shop after you've eaten, and when your energy level is high.

Make a practice of buying food in season. Check newspaper ads for sales and specialty items. Clip the ads and coupons and take them with you.

Calculate the costs of fresh, raw, frozen, canned, and dried foods. For example, canned tuna provides more protein per pound and more savings than fresh fish.

Luncheon meats at $4.48 per pound? Sliced meat at 3 ounces for $.98 adds up to a high per-pound price. Sliced meats cost more than unsliced.

Look for cheaper or generic brands; the nutritional value is usually the same. No-frills jam may contain strawberry bits instead of whole fruit, but this is not important when jam is combined with peanut butter for a sandwich.

Some generic jellies actually contain less sugar than name brands.

Save dollars by purchasing in quantity, if this is feasible for you, and pack your own groceries. Check out local food co-ops, food warehouses, and farmers' markets for fresh fruits, vegetables, eggs, and cheese. Co-ops can save you as much as 50 percent on fresh produce, 20 percent on dairy items, and 10–15 percent on other items.

Read Labels

Remember: the first ingredient listed is most plentiful. The shorter the list of ingredients, the better the product. Do not be tempted to pay $1.90 for canned water or $2.20 a pound for sugar in presweetened foods. Purchase fruits packed in their own juices. Purchase fish fresh, frozen, or packed in water or its own fish oil— *not an oil* of an unknown source.

Teach your children to read labels, too. I can hear the groans, but I suggest taking kids shopping once in a while. I have been on numerous shopping expeditions with school kids, and I know that looking at, handling, and smelling foods are sensuous learning experiences. Have them read labels and compare nutrition information. Encourage their questions and explain why you chose one brand over the other.

Be in Control

Advertisers can't make you buy anything. Leave the supermarket with what *you* need— not what the advertisers want you to need.

Do not sample foods in the store; they will whet your appetite.

Avoid shopper pitfalls: high-profit items placed in aisles and at the check-out areas, or good aromas at the deli and bakery areas. Bakery aromas are hard to resist, and retailers know it.

To avoid tantrums and harsh looks at the check-out counter when you have children with you, bring along pre-packaged healthy snacks or make trade-offs for inedible treats such as books, pens, small toys, balls, or crayons. Head for the bananas or apples—not the cupcakes and crackers.

FREEZING AHEAD: THE GREAT TIME AND MONEY SAVER

Your freezer can be a great help in saving time and money, especially if you follow one basic rule: Put the ingredients in the freezer in the form you'll be using them. If your recipes call for grated cheese or diced chicken, then grate and dice *before* you freeze. You'll be amazed at the flexibility this gives you. I even take this one step further, and actually dice the leftover chicken while my family helps with the dinner dishes. Somehow, the kitchen gets picked up, and I have a supply of ready-to-use chicken in the freezer in the same amount of time it used to take to simply do the dishes. Plus, it cuts way down on food growing old in the back of the fridge.

You'll quickly learn which freezable ingredients you use in quantity, and what are the optimum times to keep them. Basically, the colder the freezer, the better the freezer wrapping, and the shorter the stay in the freezer, the better your food will taste once thawed. And as you actively use your freezer, you'll want to label and date each item for easy, efficient retrieval.

Some Foods Freeze Better Than Others ...
Foods that freeze well include sliced meat, chicken, fish, cheese spreads, hard-boiled egg yolks, sour cream, baked beans, quiches, chives, parsley, Roquefort and bleu cheese, canned pineapple, applesauce, fruit juices,

raisins, peanut butter, catsup, chili, horse-radish, bread, nut butters, and cream cheese.

Foods that do not freeze well include hard-boiled egg whites, cottage cheese, tomatoes, celery, cucumbers, green peppers, lettuce, watercress, cabbage, radishes, carrots, onions, apples, mayonnaise, salad dressings, jellies, jams and preserves, liver sausage, luncheon meats, pimento, and pickles.

FREEZING SANDWICHES
Sandwiches can be prepared in advance and frozen without becoming soggy if you take precautions to keep all moisture away from the bread. Here's how.

★ Spread the bread with a good protective coating of butter, corn oil margarine, or peanut butter to prevent fillings from soaking into the bread. Spread both slices all the way to the edges.

★ Don't add lettuce, tomatoes, carrots, or other raw veggies, as well as mustard or mayonnaise, to sandwiches before freezing. (Actually, these are best when sent in separate wrappers to be added to the sandwich right before eating.)

★ Sandwiches should be packed in freezer-wrap (plastic wrap won't do) or moisture-proof containers. Eat freezer sandwiches within two weeks if stored at 0 degrees F., or use within one week if stored in the freezer compartment of the refrigerator.

SANDWICHES THAT FREEZE WELL

Cooked chicken, turkey, fish, ham, salami, beef, and pork. These are especially good when mixed with sour cream, yogurt, buttermilk, creamy-style salad dressings, chili seasoning, catsup, applesauce, or fruit juice.

Spicy Ham. Blend 4 ounces diced ham with 1 tablespoon pickle relish.

Cran-chicken. Combine 1 cup diced cooked chicken or turkey with 2 tablespoons of cranberry-orange relish.

Nutty Cheese. Add ¼ pound finely chopped walnuts to ¼ pound grated Swiss or American cheese. Mix with paprika-butter spread (made from the recipe for Basic Spreadables on page 55).

Sardine and Egg. Mix equal parts sardines and hard-boiled egg yolks with salt, paprika, and mustard to taste. Thin to a paste by adding a little lemon juice.

Mexican Bean Spread. Combine 1 cup mashed cold baked beans with 2 tablespoons chile con carne seasoning and 2 teaspoons minced onion.

WRAPPING FOR THE FREEZER

For packing and freezing sandwiches or meats, the old-fashioned drugstore wrap is unbeatable. Place the sandwich in the center of a piece of foil or freezer-wrap paper large enough to easily cover the sandwich and allow for a double-fold seam on the edges. Fold the seam tightly and turn the package so that the seam is on the underside. Fold the ends into a triangle, carefully forcing out excess air. Double-fold the triangle to form sealing points. Fold ends over and seal with freezer tape.

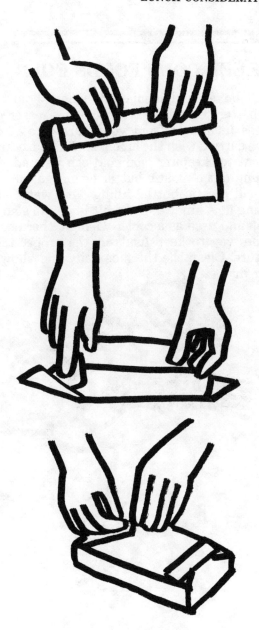

KEEP COLD FOODS COLD

Lunch boxes and insulated carriers hold the cold better than plain brown bags. Freezer gel devices (available from your hardware store) can be carried with the lunch. A simple freezing element for keeping food cold can be made by cleaning out a plastic butter or margarine tub or small plastic bottle, filling with water and freezing it. A small can of fruit juice can also be frozen and used as a cooler. Using a thermos is a good way to keep foods at the proper temperature. Clean the thermos daily and allow it to air dry.

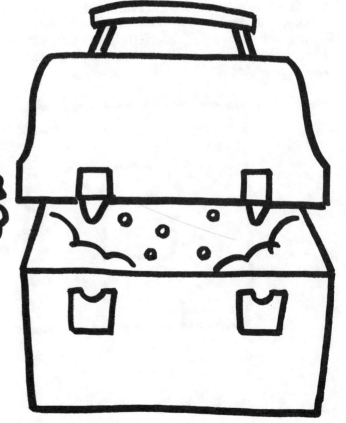

PACK IT RIGHT!

Even family favorites won't get eaten if they look unappetizing by lunchtime. Actually, packing portable meals well involves a lot of common sense, mixed with a bit of humor — two things in short supply during morning rush hours. So here are a few tips that will go a long way toward helping you pack it right.

SUPPLIES

Keep a good supply of plastic wrap, foil, twist ties, sandwich bags, plastic forks, knives, and spoons . . . and, of course, lunch-size brown bags.

Consider investing in a good wide-mouth thermos (without a glass liner if kids are using it), a plastic sandwich-size container (wonderful solution to the smushed sandwich problem), and a few half-pint covered plastic containers (if you don't have a supply from reuseable margarine tubs, etc.).

Save margarine tubs, styrofoam containers with hinged lids, plastic cups with lids. Remember not to put plastic containers and lids in the dishwasher, as they don't seal well after that.

FOODS

Keep the obvious in mind: hot foods hot; cold foods cold; crisp foods crisp.

Separate foods as much as possible. Garnishes, sandwich toppings, salad dressings should all be packed separately to be added at lunchtime. Most "extras" can simply be tucked in individual sandwich bags.

Foods with strong odors often aren't the best totables. If you do pack them, they need to be packed in containers with tight seals.

A can of frozen fruit or fruit juice makes an excellent natural cooler, and one less thing to carry home.

SPECIAL CONSIDERATIONS FOR KIDS

Don't insist that your child carry a lunchbox if brown bags are "in" this year. Peer pressure exerts itself even in this area, so listen to what your child says.

Include extras of crisp veggies or not-too-sweet desserts, so your child can *share* rather than *trade*.

Look at what comes back in the lunchbox, and ask, without being defensive, why it wasn't eaten.

Communicate about lunchtime. Who'd you eat with? Where did you eat? Did you have enough time today? Did you like your lunch today? are important questions.

Learn the favorites, and prepare them frequently as you gradually introduce new foods.

Cut sandwiches in various sizes and shapes—younger children like shapes made with large-sized cookie cutters.

Toss in granola, popcorn, or nut balls.

Decorate sandwiches and cookies with a smiling raisin face, an initial, or a big X for a kiss.

For holidays, pack special napkins, straws, or plates.

And for kids of all ages, tuck in a note, sticker, puzzle, riddle, clipping, cartoon, or flower. You'll make their day!

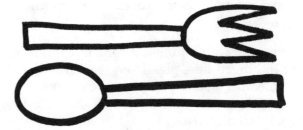

MISCELLANEOUS PRACTICALITIES

★ Limit the number of reuseable containers you send along to one to two.

★ Be sure lids are tight-fitting and screwed on tightly. On the other hand, be sure they can be opened again at lunchtime!

★ Avoid glass containers.

★ Put a name and address on lunch boxes, satchels, brown bags.

★ Introduce new food slowly, not more than one new item a day.

★ Match the container to the food. Not only will the lunch look and taste better, but this will help avoid embarrassing cafeteria accidents.

PACK NUTRITION IN YOUR BAG

We hear so much these days about good nutrition and about developing good eating habits that we often lose track of the meaning of the goals. Basically if we eat more of what is good for us, and less of what is harmful for us, we will feel better, function better, and look better. It's as simple as that.

BASIC NUTRITION KNOW-HOW

Most of us have a clear idea of what is good for us in our diets, and though we may be confused about specifically which foods are harmful, we are generally aware that we should avoid too much sugar, salt, and fats. How do you translate this general awareness into packing healthful lunches?

Ask yourself, "What is a good lunch?" Definitely, one that is *eaten*. Lunch tossed away or given away does no good and is the most expensive of all meals. Generally the midday meal should provide one-third of the day's needs for calories, proteins, vitamins, and minerals.

A HEALTHFUL LUNCH CONTAINS ...
Protein-Rich Foods. Meat, fish, cheese, eggs, peanut butter, chicken, tofu, turkey, dried beans, peas, and legumes in combination with grains are good sources of protein.

Nutrition-wise people stretch proteins by mixing and matching the sources of their proteins. Protein from beans is better utilized by your body if some animal food (milk) or cereal food (bread) is also eaten. Other good protein combinations are:

★ Meat with baked beans

Peanut butter with wheat bread

Pork with cheese

Chicken with egg noodles

Tofu (the soybean cheese) with yogurt or quiche

Eggs with sardines, tuna, tortillas

Fish or seafood with potatoes

Cheese with walnuts

Bean soup with sesame seeds

★ Falafel (chickpeas) with pita bread

Vegetables. Those rich in vitamin A (dark salad greens, leafy vegetables, carrots, sweet potatoes) and vitamin C (tomatoes, broccoli, green peppers, cabbage) are especially important.

Fruits. Apricots, pineapple, oranges, apples, grapefruit, tangerines, cherries, grapes, berries, melons, and bananas make good lunchtime eating.

Whole Grain Breads. Whole wheat, rye, cracked wheat, oat, and wheat berry are inexpensive sources of vitamin B, iron, and important fiber.

Calcium-Rich Foods. Yogurt, tofu, kefir, milk, cheese, and non-fat dry milk are good sources of calcium.

Select fresh green vegetables to protect against infection while providing high vitamin and mineral counts. For a quick, low-cal soup, cook a favorite vegetable until tender. Blend the vegetable and cooking water together. Add skim milk and heat gently. Sip slowly.

Charge up your immune system with mineral-rich foods. For *calcium*, have plenty of milk, dairy products, dark leafy veggies, nuts, sardines, yogurt, and sesame seeds. *Magnesium* can be found in almonds, dried fruit, beans, bananas, potatoes, and spinach. Whole grains, especially wheat germ, oats, and corn, as well as seafood, meat, and eggs are good sources of *zinc*. *Vitamin C*, which encourages the body to combat and destroy viruses, is found in fruits, cabbage, broccoli, bean sprouts, seeds, bell peppers, and strawberries. For a protecting boost, stir ½ teaspoon of vitamin C powder into fruit and vegetable juices.

"SUPER FOODS" FOR TOP NUTRITION

I call foods that furnish major health bonuses "super foods." They contain nutrients essential for keeping the body young—protein for growth and repair; complex carbohydrates for steady endurance and fiber; fatty acids to keep skin, hair, nails, and membranes healthy; natural sugars for energy; vitamins for body regulators; and minerals to keep digestion running smoothly. Super foods that pack the most nutrition for the number of calories include the following:

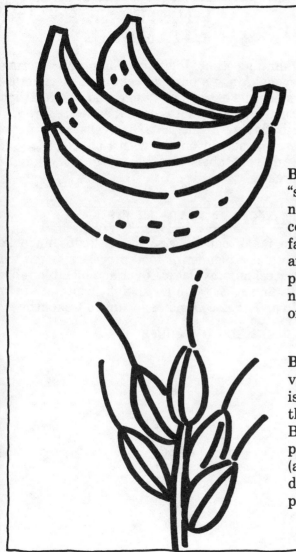

Bananas. The original wrapper-food contains "super" potassium, so essential for heart and nerve functions, as well as muscle contractions. Bananas contain practically no fat. They furnish fiber; vitamins A, B, and C; and some calcium and phosphorus. Bananas please all palates, having about 29 percent natural sugar and 90–100 calories, depending on their size.

Brown Rice. Brown rice contains the nutty, vitamin-rich hull of the natural grain, which is loaded with B vitamins, especially thiamine, so essential for healthy nerves. Brown rice also packs potassium, some protein, complex carbohydrates, and niacin (another B vitamin). Combine brown rice with dried mushrooms, carrots, green and red peppers, and spices for an Oriental treat.

ATHLETES NEED VITAMIN B2

Pumping iron? Jogging? Taking an afternoon swim? Make a habit of taking in extra milk or spoonfuls of yogurt. People who exercise vigorously 30–50 minutes each day need extra B2 – riboflavin – a nutrient that cells need for energy. Fuel up on B2 with rich yogurt, green leafy vegetables, lean meats, eggs, and fortified bread.

MAKING OAT FLOUR

To make oat flour, place 1½ cups uncooked oats in a blender or food processor fitted with a steel mixing blade. Cover and blend for about 1 minute. Store in an airtight container in the freezer or a cool place for up to 6 months.

MAKES ABOUT 1¼ CUPS

Dried Beans. This is one of the super sources of protein and complex carbohydrates, fiber for lowering cholesterol, calcium, phosphorus, and potassium—even some iron. Beans also pack B vitamins thiamine, riboflavin, niacin, and pyridoxine. Eating 4 ounces of beans a day lowers blood cholesterol 9 percent and contributes only 150 calories.

Eggs. One large egg contains 80 calories and packs a nutritional dose of 98 percent assimilated protein; vitamins A, B, and E; calcium; and phosphorus. Hard-boiled in their shells, eggs make quick, versatile, low-calorie, and low-cost snacks. The yolk contains a rich source of sulfur—the mineral needed for healthy skin, hair, and nails.

Oats. For "feeling your oats," fuel up with oatmeal. One ounce of cooked oatmeal contains 110 calories, much protein, vitamins B and E, iron, calcium, silicon (the beauty mineral), magnesium, and potassium. Low in sodium, oats act as a fat trap for the heart and are a super source of fiber (even better than wheat fiber).

Oat flakes can be added to hamburgers, meat loaves, soups, stews, and spaghetti and pizza sauces as a nutritional enhancer. Toss a handful of oat flour into cookies, cakes, breads, and fruit desserts.

LOWERING THE SUGAR CONTENT IN YOUR FOODS

Too much refined sugar in the diet has been linked to tooth decay, obesity, heart disease, hypoglycemia, diabetes, allergies, and hyperactivity, in addition to other health-related problems.

In nature, sugar is packaged with fiber, vitamins, and minerals—as in a banana. A banana may provide the same glucose as a candy bar, but the process by which the body assimilates the glucose differs. Sucrose from candy is poured into the body quickly, while fructose (fruit sugar) dribbles in more slowly, protected by fiber, vitamins, and minerals.

Substitute popcorn, fruit, raw vegetables, granola, nut and fruit mix, dry roasted nuts, unshelled nuts, yogurt, pure juices, and melons for sugary sweets. (Fruit Pops are always popular with young people. See page 178.)

Bake your own cookies, breads, and cakes when possible, using polyunsaturated vegetable oil, skim milk, and low-fat buttermilk. Use as sugar substitutes ripe mashed bananas, raisins, coconut, grated carrots or zucchini, pumpkin, cranberries, dates, chopped apples, and molasses. Also use whole wheat flour, bran, and wheat germ.

By making your own cookies and cakes you can control the kind of fat and the amount of sweetener. Most recipes and commercial bakery products use saturated fat and could stand a 25–50 percent reduction in sugar. (For more information on healthful cookies and cakes, see Chapter 9.)

AVOID TOOTH ROBBERS

All sugar, refined processed foods, and artificially colored soft drinks are bad for the teeth. "Forget" to bring home high-calorie, sugary, caffeine-laced drinks. Many parents justify purchasing soft drinks, cookies, and candy by "buying them for the kids;" then they watch in dismay as the kids gobble up the sweets. Don't blame the kids.

ENCOURAGE TOOTH PROTECTORS

Buy fresh fruits, vegetables, proteins, grains, and nuts.

Dentists urge parents to read labels and not to purchase foods with added sugar—dextrose, sucrose, or glucose. When reading labels, remember first is most. If sugar is listed as one of the first four items on the label, try to find an alternative. If you can't pronounce it, don't test it on kids.

LOWERING SALT CONTENT

Have you ever noticed how quickly lettuce or cucumbers wilt when sprinkled with salt? Their cells collapse as salt draws out the water. Excessive use of salt contributes to high blood pressure, hypertension, obesity, kidney diseases, and premenstrual irritability.

Try cutting in half the amount of salt used in cooking, then cut in half again. Explore flavoring alternatives such as dry mustard, herbs, spices, curry, cumin, lemon, lime juice, and vinegars.

Choose garlic powder instead of garlic salt and celery powder over celery salt. Use chili seasoning not chili powder. Make friends with parsley, water chestnuts, and peppercorns.

Look for less salty or low-sodium foods when shopping. When salt or sodium is listed as one of the first items on a label, seek out alternatives. Processed cheese spreads are twice as salty as natural cheddar cheese. Prepared French or Italian dressing may be four times as salty as mayonnaise. Soy sauce has four to six times the salt as the same amount of catsup. Fresh green peas contain 2 milligrams of sodium per half cup. When peas are canned, the sodium increases to 236 milligrams.

Use unsalted dry cottage cheese, horseradish, or tabasco. Cooking wine contains sodium; table wine does not.

Watch out for hidden sodium in foods. An ounce of corn flakes has more sodium than an ounce of salted peanuts, and a half cup of chocolate pudding has more sodium than three slices of bacon. I can't stress enough the importance of reading labels.

Bouillon cubes, Worcestershire, MSG, and brine are too high in sodium for healthy eaters.

Substitute Vegetable Salt for table salt in recipes and on the table.

VEGETABLE SALT
(A SALT SUBSTITUTE)

3 ounces dry mixed vegetables, pulverized
¼ teaspoon garlic powder
⅛ teaspoon dried thyme
¼ teaspoon white onion powder
¼ teaspoon green onion powder
¼ teaspoon paprika
⅛ teaspoon ground celery seed
¼ teaspoon dry mustard
½ teaspoon dried parsley, pulverized
¼ teaspoon dried red and green peppers, pulverized

Combine all ingredients in a blender and process until well mixed. Place in a portable shaker.

LOWERING FAT CONTENT

Too much fat in the diet is also a health hazard.

Purchase only lean cuts of meat and remove all fat before cooking. Avoid marbled meat. Broil, braise, or grill meat to allow fat to drip off. Chilling meat hardens fat and makes it easier to remove. Fish is lower in total fat than meat or poultry. Round, London broil, pot roast, flank steak, and sirloin are lower in fat than other cuts of beef. Hamburger ground from any of these cuts is also leaner. Pre-ground hamburger contains fats even when labeled "lean."

Remove the high-fat skin from poultry before cooking. Select young turkeys and chickens for less fat. White turkey meat is leaner than dark meat.

Switch to dry curd cottage cheese, low-fat yogurt, tofu, buttermilk, non-fat dry milk, and kefir (a cultured milk product similar to yogurt) for salad dressings and sauces. Substituting yogurt for sour cream saves 335 calories per cup, an 83 percent reduction of fat.

Enjoy farmer, ricotta, Swiss, pot, hoop, skim-milk, low-salt, and low-fat cheeses. Take mini-nibbles of other cheeses. (Kefir cheese is delicious—low in fat and calories.)

Experiment with carob, which contains 2 percent fat, compared to chocolate, which contains 52 percent fat.

Select safflower, corn, sesame, sunflower, or peanut oil. Use oils or nut butters without added sugar, hydrogenated fats, or preservatives.

Skip the salad dressing to save 10 pounds a year (each tablespoon adds 100 calories). Top salads with marinated vegetables instead of salad dressings.

Get acquainted with tofu—the soybean cheese that is high in protein, low in fat, and extremely inexpensive. Tofu is bland tasting when eaten by itself, but takes on the flavor of the food it is mixed with, making it perfect for stretching and nutritionally enhancing salad dressings, sauces, dips, soups, and cheese and meat dishes.

FREE TOFU RECIPES

Nature's Touch Soyfoods will send you tofu recipes free of charge. Just mail a self-addressed, stamped envelope to Nature's Touch Recipes, Box N511, Encinitas, California 92024.

A sample recipe is Light Burgers, which is made with a ratio of two parts ground beef to one part regular-style tofu. Mash the tofu in a large bowl, add the ground beef, and season. Combine thoroughly. Cook the same as all-beef burgers. Light Burgers cut costs by 16 percent, fat by 26 percent, calories by 24 percent, and cholesterol by 33 percent. The burgers stay plump and moist, and each cooked 4-ounce patty contains 22 grams of protein.

LUNCH CAN BE FUN, TOO!

You will know your lunch has passed the what's-right-for-lunch test when your youngster asks you to pack an extra for a friend. Here are some ideas.

Vegetables come in an array of bright colors, and the crunchy ones please the tooth fairy. Totable vegetable munchies include cherry tomatoes, celery chunks, carrot rolls, and cauliflower florets. Spurned vegetables become yummy when a tangy dip is packed as a go-along. Super salads can be tossed with favorite vegetables and topped with raisins and nuts.

For kids who hate eggs, try hard-boiling them and letting each child color his or her own. Or use a felt-tipped pen to draw a funny face on the egg.

Alphabet noodles in soup entice kids and make both eating lunch and learning fun.

THE COLLECTIBLE LUNCHBOX

The Thermos Company has been making lunch boxes for 50 years and Aladdin for 25. Now these lunch boxes are becoming collectible items at garage sales, yard sales, and thrift shops. Collectors are interested in these lunch boxes as examples of American art and are driving up prices in New York and Los Angeles to between $25 and $50 per box—minus the thermos!

So take care of that lunch box.

GET KIDS INTO THE ACT

If you are a mom or dad and are making brown bag lunches for your kids (and maybe yourself, too), you know how finicky kids can be. You begin to learn that sandwiches made on dark bread are traded for just about anything on white bread; egg sandwiches seem to always be traded for jam sandwiches. What's a parent to do? Here's a secret for adding nutrition to kids' lunches: *Foods prepared by kids themselves rarely go uneaten.* You can channel kids' energies and appetites by involving them in preparing and packing nutritious lunches.

Having done thousands of simple classroom cooking projects at schools, I've learned that kids usually eat what they prepare—"even a lumpy failure." Kids who have never eaten whole wheat bread will eat loaves that they bake themselves and have fun telling you, "I made it myself." In addition to providing an edible reward, cooking provides kids with a real sense of accomplishment and a healthy outlet for tension and emotional frustrations.

Even very young children enjoy stirring bread, scraping carrots, washing lettuce, and getting the ingredients from the refrigerator. Kids are great at patching up a recipe, inventing a new one, or giving an old one a new twist. They discover new skills, tastes, textures, and food combinations while having fun.

Face-Me-Funny Sandwiches are decorated to tempt taste buds. A plain sandwich can be uninteresting. Use your imagination to "face one funny" and let the kids get into the act. Decorate an open-faced peanut butter sandwich with eyes of sliced olives or carrots and white raisins for the pupil of the eye. A thin strip of green pepper is the mouth, pimento strips for the eyebrows, grapes for the nose, shredded coconut or alfalfa sprouts for the fringy hair. Kids love to decorate with nuts, sunflower seeds, apricots, fresh apples, mung bean sprouts, carob bits, and radish slices.

GOOD NUTRITION AND WEIGHT CONTROL GO TOGETHER!

One of the nicest things about developing good nutritional habits is that good nutrition goes hand-in-hand with weight control. For those who find they are constantly fighting weight gain, or are concerned about weight gain in their spouse or children, packing a nutritionally sound lunch becomes increasingly significant. All too often, poorly planned lunches or lunches that consist of fast food or grabbing something on-the-go result in many, many "empty" calories.

You can "fat-proof" your house by buying only healthful foods and planning ahead for snack attacks. But if you don't carry this approach to weight-conscious eating outside your home

into your portable lunches, you'll feel that you've lost the battle. Remember, you'll want an appealing lunch every day, not a carrot stick one day and a piece of chocolate cake the next.

Obesity generally runs in families. When one parent is overweight, there is a 40 percent chance that the kids will be also. When both parents are overweight, the odds jump to 80 percent.

Sometimes parents confuse giving love with giving the most—the most attention, the most devoted care, and the most food. Fat kids are not fit or healthy, and they are teased, rejected, and ridiculed, which certainly does not help them develop positive self-images.

How can parents raise fat-free kids? "Fat-proofed" kids begin with parents who are fit and trim themselves. Between the ages of 2 and 6 years kids imitate parents and peers. Mom and Dad cannot munch on Marshmallow Fairies and expect Tommy and Mary to eat sugarless treats.

If the whole family turns to nutritionally sound, lower-calorie eating, the children will regard this as standard behavior. For overweight children, emphasize the normality of good eating, rather than dwelling on what they shouldn't or can't eat. And be sure to pack appealing lunches that don't appear dietetic, but are instead fun and filling. A puzzle or sticker goes a long way to replace calorie laden desserts, and makes your child feel very special indeed!

TEENS NEED HELP WITH NUTRITION

As kids get older, you may feel that they are more influenced by what other kids are eating than by your concerns for their nutritional well-being.

Try not to make a big issue over their eating habits. You don't want to alienate them and be ignored. Instead enlist their help and work with their expressed likes and dislikes.

Involve older kids in making decisions about packing nutrient-rich foods, balanced with some less valuable goodies. Offer choices, such as a spinach salad with mushrooms or a carrot salad. You may get one eaten because they've participated in the decision-making.

Vary the lunches, so lunch doesn't get dull. Alternate salads, soups, and sandwiches to perk up appetites.

For teenagers, who often seem ravenous at all times, don't get into a lecture on how much they seem to eat. Just be sure to provide nutritious choices for them to fuel their adolescent bodies. Focus on good foods rather than when or where they eat.

Have teenagers help in preparing vegetables in a wok. Stir-fried vegetables are crisp, colorful, nutritious, and delicious, plus teens seem to approve of this kind of cooking. It's a good way to get some help in the kitchen as well as get veggies eaten.

Some kids just don't like milk, so work with them on this. For reluctant milk drinkers, try shakes or blender smoothies (see page 145). Custards or puddings are healthy alternatives for providing adequate calcium, and are welcome additions to a portable lunch. Or add non-fat dry milk powder to meat loaves, soups, cookies, muffins and cakes. Every teaspoon of non-fat dry milk provides 50 milligrams of calcium and no fat. Sprinkle calcium-rich sesame seeds on salads or use as soup floaters.

LOW-CALORIE TIPS FOR BROWN BAGGERS

★ Go "no frills" while upping nutrients. Skimp on condiments such as butter, mayonnaise, salad oils, gravies, sauces, and sour cream. Choose a medium-size baked potato, one small bran muffin, 1½ slices of American cheese, or 4 ounces of vanilla or lemon yogurt. (An 8-ounce carton of cottage cheese or yogurt equals two servings, not one.)

★ Educate your taste buds. One brand of low-fat yogurt contains 2 grams of fat and 240 calories, while one that is not low-fat weighs in with 4 to 6 grams of fat and 270 calories. Cottage cheese calories also vary from 90 to 120 in an 8-ounce container. Again, check your labels.

★ Switch to *plain* low-fat yogurt and save as much as 350 calories per cup. Stir a tablespoon of fruit concentrate in for added flavor.

★ Combine plain yogurt and frozen unsweetened berries in a blender for a frozen yogurt treat.

★ Use fresh fruit compote as a topping for yogurt, cottage cheese, and cookies. Mix 4 cups of fresh fruit with ¾ cup orange juice and store in the refrigerator for snack attacks.

★ Switch to lower-butterfat cream cheese or replace cream cheese with farmer cheese, ricotta, or Neufchatel cheese.

★ Blender-whip fresh farmer cheese or low-fat cottage cheese smooth as a substitute for cream cheese in cheesecakes.

★ Make sandwich cookies by spreading graham crackers with farmer cheese or low-fat cream cheese and sliced strawberries rather than strawberry jam. Switch to peanut butter and no jelly—use fruit or berries instead.

★ Mix frozen unsweetened berries with skim milk for a frosty milkshake. For a Skinny Frappe, blend together ⅓ cup non-fat dry milk, ½ cup water, 6 ice cubes, 2 teaspoons vanilla extract, and ½ medium-size banana.

★ Serve fruit or melon wedges for sweet treats.

★ Convert to fruit instead of sugar to add flavor and nutrition. Substitute dried fruits, fruit concentrates, and juices for sugar in recipes (see page 50).

★ Use defatted or dry-roasted nuts. Crush nuts on top of a recipe rather than inside a batter—you use less.

★ Surprise your taste buds by using more vanilla and sweet spices, such as cinnamon, nutmeg, and ginger.

★ Use a single pie crust and save 800 calories per pie.

★ Switch to plain gelatin desserts and control portions to prevent large servings.

★ Push vegetables and fruits. Sneak leftover spurned vegetables into soup, stews, pizza, and spaghetti sauces. Grate carrots or zucchini and add to muffins or waffles. Serve skinnywiches topless with sprouts, letting dark leafy greens replace one slice of bread.

★ Make every sandwich a little skinnier by slicing bread extra thin.

★ Instead of eating packaged, fried, salted corn chips, make your own toasted chips from dairy-case or pre-packaged tortillas cut into 6–8 wedges each. Spread them in a single layer on a cookie sheet and bake at 400°F. for 10–12 minutes. Dust lightly with chili seasoning while still warm.

TOO THIN CAN POSE A PROBLEM, TOO!

Underweight people's eating habits do not gain as much attention as diets for their overweight friends, since obesity is considered a major health hazard. However, recent research has shown that being too thin may shorten life expectancy even more than being too fat. School kids who are too thin are the envy of their heavier friends, yet they tend to be self-conscious about their weight, too, and have problems getting clothes to fit. Underweight kids may lack energy to compete in sports—eating enough to maintain body weight in addition to the extra two or three thousand calories for active sports can be a terrific problem.

Remember to follow good nutritional guidelines, and avoid empty calories here, too. This is weight control from the other end of the spectrum, but you'll still want to avoid too much salt, refined sugar, and fat.

TIPS FOR THE UNDERWEIGHT PERSON'S EATING PLAN

★ Include high caloric foods for meals and snacks. Recommended oils for dressings, baking, stir-frying, and spreads include corn, safflower, sunflower, and peanut.

★ Do not eat salads or vegetables first before a meal—treat them as extra side dishes in order not to be appetite spoilers. Spoon on nuts, croutons, salad dressing, or cheese toppings.

★ Load up on rice, pasta, pizza, potatoes, dry beans, and fruit breads.

★ Snack before bedtime on peanut butter and banana sandwiches, cookies, fresh fruit yogurt, sesame sticks, milk shakes, muffins, crackers, cheese, or flavored popcorn.

★ Plan for "mini" eating—midmorning and midafternoon meals, as well as breakfast, lunch, and dinner.

★ Relax and enjoy exercise, which often helps a skinny person's appetite to improve.

MAKE NUTRITION FUN

Whatever meal you are considering, be sure that nutrition is in your bag. Packing meals for healthy eating may require changing your food habits by eliminating frills; cutting down on sugar, fat, and salt; increasing fiber by using whole foods; and learning to read labels.

May this book help you to pack meals easily, economically, and nutritiously.

SANDWICHES

PITA POCKETS, TERRIFIC TACOS, AND OLD FAVORITES UPDATED

Whether they are packing for a school lunch, an afternoon party, or a fishing trip, brown baggers know that sandwiches are the number one favorite for packing convenience, nutrition, and good taste. Even if your favorite sandwich is peanut butter, tuna, cheese, sandwich meat, or a BLT, you'll find some recipes here for variations on a theme, new spreads, and creative combinations to prevent the "same-old-sandwich" blues. Be adventurous! Try a new taste, a new shape, or a new texture, and bring your lunch to life.

Begin by taking a new look at the traditional sandwich breads—sandwich fillings don't have to sit on those same old familiar two slices. Consider using whole wheat English muffins, onion bagels, sandwich-size pita breads, a variety of flavored and sized crackers, or any of the widely available specialty breads, such as sprouted wheat or wheat and raisin. Think, too, about creating sandwiches with only one slice of bread, topped with a large lettuce leaf. Or make a sandwich with no bread at all—just roll your favorite fillings in lettuce leaves or thin cheese slices. Experiment by taking an old favorite like peanut butter or tuna salad, and trying it on a new bread; you're in for a pleasant surprise!

PEANUT BUTTER: THE SUPER SPREADABLE

If you're thinking, who needs a cookbook to make a peanut butter and jelly sandwich (even if it is on a raisin bagel), you're right. But if I can nudge you along to think of peanut butter as a wonderfully nutritious food that can be oh-so-versatile too, then you'll see why I give it so much emphasis.

Peanut butter packs a nutritional wallop with 24 grams of protein in 4½ tablespoons. Peanut butter protein is increased when served on whole grain bread and accompanied by a glass of milk. Just 1 pound has the total nutrient equivalent to 1.4 pounds of cheese, 2.5 pounds of steak, 4 quarts of milk, or 32 eggs.

NOT ALL PEANUT BUTTER IS CREATED EQUAL

When purchasing peanut butter, be sure to purchase a brand with no added sweeteners or emulsifiers. (Sucrose, dextrose, sugar, and molasses are all sweeteners.) One tablespoon of peanut butter can contain as much as ⅔ teaspoon of sugar; adding 2 tablespoons of grape jelly packs an additional 3¾ teaspoons of sugar!

The best peanut butter—best-tasting and best for you—is the peanut butter you grind yourself. Health food stores and many supermarkets have grinders right next to the barrels of unsalted peanuts, so be particular and grind

Keep individual containers of carrots, celery, zucchini, cucumber strips, green pepper rings, turnip chunks, radishes, and tomato wedges in the refrigerator ready to be added to the lunch box right before leaving the house. Vary the shapes of raw vegetables.

PEANUT BUTTER SPROUTWICH

¼ cup shredded lettuce mixed with
    alfalfa sprouts
1 tablespoon lemon juice
1 tablespoon toasted sesame seeds
1 tablespoon cranberry sauce or
    cranberry relish
4 tablespoons peanut butter
2 slices date bread
2 strips bacon, cooked crisp and drained

Mix the lettuce and sprouts with the lemon juice and sesame seeds. Pack the lettuce and sprout mixture separately to place on the sandwich when ready to eat. Pack the cranberry sauce in a small container with lid. Spread the peanut butter on the bread. Top with the bacon slices. Pack. At lunchtime, open the sandwich and top with the alfalfa mixture and cranberry sauce.

1 SERVING

PEANUT BUTTER AND TOFU SANDWICH

6 ounces tofu
½ cup peanut butter
1 banana
1 tablespoon lemon juice
2 tablespoons applesauce
2 slices raisin bread

Place the tofu, peanut butter, banana, lemon juice, and applesauce in a blender or food processor and process until smooth. Spoon filling for 1 sandwich into a wide-mouth thermos. Pack 2 slices of raisin bread in sandwich bag. Store extra spread in the refrigerator.

1 SERVING

PEANUT BUTTER AND EGG SANDWICH

3–4 tablespoons peanut butter
1–2 teaspoons pickle relish, well-drained
1   hard-boiled egg, sliced
Salad greens
2   slices wheat berry bread

Spread one slice of wheat berry bread with peanut butter. Top with 1 or 2 teaspoons of well-drained pickle relish. Layer on slices of hard-boiled eggs. Top with the second slice of bread. Place in a sandwich container. Pack salad greens in a separate container for adding to the sandwich when ready to eat.

1 SERVING

PEANUT BUTTER SUNSHINE SANDWICH

½ cup peanut butter
4 ounces cream cheese, softened
4 tablespoons orange juice concentrate
1 tablespoon grated carrots
1 tablespoon diced raisins, dates, or
     currants
4 slices whole grain bread

Mix the peanut butter, orange juice, carrots, cream cheese, and raisins. Spread on the bread.

2 SERVINGS

PEANUT BUTTER SPREAD

½ cup peanut butter
¼ cup orange juice concentrate
1 teaspoon grated orange peel
⅓ cup grated carrots

Mix all the ingredients and spread on bread or crackers.

MAKES 1 CUP

CHICKEN AND HAM SPREAD

Put leftover pieces of chicken and ham through a meat grinder or chop in a food processor. Add Worcestershire sauce and enough yogurt to make it spreadable.

TOFU SPREAD

Juice of ½ lemon
2   tablespoons wine vinegar
½   garlic clove, minced
1   teaspoon brown mustard
½   cup safflower mayonnaise
1   teaspoon tamari
1½ cups cubed tofu
2   tablespoons sesame oil
3   tablespoons plain yogurt

Place all the ingredients in a blender or food processor and process until smooth. If the mixture is too thick, thin with additional yogurt. Store in the refrigerator.

MAKES ABOUT 2¼ CUPS

COOL CUCUMBER SPREAD

¾   cup cottage cheese, low-fat
¼   cup diced cucumber
3   tablespoons minced parsley
2   dozen triangles of wheat or oatmeal bread

Blend all ingredients except the bread, spread on 12 triangles of bread and cover with the remaining bread triangles. Garnish with tiny wedges of cucumber or baby pickles.

1 DOZEN TRIANGLES

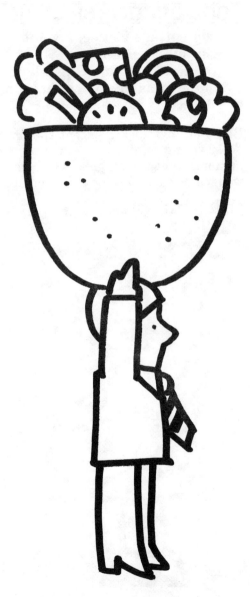

PITA POCKET PORTABLES

Pita bread is a natural for portable lunches. In fact, pita bread provides a whole new array of possibilities for sandwiches because just about everything can be stuffed into a pocket — tossed salads, thick stews, pilafs. Mix sandwich regulars with some new ingredients. Turn leftovers into pita feasts (send pockets in plastic bags, hot fillings in a wide-mouth thermos).

Make a nontraditional pita taco — your favorite taco fillings scooped into a pocket. And don't overlook pockets lined with nut butters and then filled with fresh veggies. Or introduce hummus to your menu, a protein-rich spread of puréed chick-peas, tahini, and lemon juice. Fill your pocket with Hummus (page 56), topped with chopped egg and sprouts, and you have an unbelievable treat.

Some favorite pita bread fillings (almost anything goes):

Thinly sliced chicken with:

★ Chunks of red or green pepper, yogurt, and chutney.

★ Celery, pickle, and your favorite seasonings.

★ Hard-boiled egg, pimento, and mayonnaise.

★ Apple, pickle, and sesame spread.

★ Chopped nuts, celery powder, and lemon juice.

Slivers of roast beef with:

★ Sliced cherry tomatoes, chopped scallions, and cubes of low-fat cream cheese, topped with alfalfa sprouts.

★ Crisp, crumbled bacon with: Diced tomato, shredded lettuce, and plain yogurt.

Hard-boiled eggs with:

★ Mayonnaise, minced onion, and crumbled blue cheese.

Falafel with:

★ Herbed yogurt dressing, chopped tomatoes and cucumbers, alfalfa sprouts, and a dollop of kefir cheese.

★ Guacamole with grated carrot and zucchini, diced tomatoes, and horseradish, topped with alfalfa sprouts and grated Monterey jack cheese.

★ Tofu, avocado slices, tomato cubes, chopped scallions, dash of cayenne, alfalfa sprouts, and sunflower seeds.

PITA SALAD SANDWICH

1   pita bread round
2   ounces cooked turkey strips
⅓   cup chopped lettuce
¼   tomato, diced
2   tablespoons chopped onion
3   tablespoons plain yogurt
¼   teaspoon garlic powder
⅛   teaspoon dry mustard
⅛   teaspoon curry powder

Wrap the pita bread in a plastic bag. Pack the turkey with the chopped lettuce, tomato, and onion. Mix the yogurt and seasonings and pack in a small covered container. At lunchtime, combine the turkey and vegetables with the yogurt in the pita bread pocket.

1 SERVING

VEGETARIAN PEANUTTY PITA

1   teaspoon peanut butter
½   cup plain yogurt
½   cup shredded lettuce
½   medium-size tomato, coarsely chopped
¼   medium-size cucumber, coarsely chopped
2   sweet red onion slices
1   pita bread round
Handful of low-sodium peanuts

Combine the peanut butter and yogurt. Pack in one container. Bag the lettuce, tomatoes, cucumbers, and onion slices together. Bag the sprouts separately. Wrap the pita in a plastic bag. At eating time, stuff the pita pocket with the vegetable mixture, pour on the peanut-yogurt dressing, and top with sprouts and peanuts.

1 SERVING

TACOS

Tacos are becoming fast food favorites, and they make good portable lunches, too. You have a choice here in how you pack them. You can send taco shells wrapped in plastic bags with the ingredients in separate containers. The shells, frankly, don't always make it in one piece, but they taste just as good crunched on top of the filling—more like a taco-flavored stew. Or, as the kids certainly perfer, send along a pita pocket for all the taco fillings. Works well and tastes great!

MEAT TACOS

¼   **pound lean ground beef**
¼   **cup mild taco sauce**
1   **cup grated Monterey jack or cheddar cheese**
½   **cup diced tomatoes**
½   **cup shredded lettuce**
½   **cup alfalfa sprouts**
2   **corn taco shells or 2 pita pockets**

Brown the beef in a nonstick pan; drain thoroughly. Stir in the taco sauce and heat well. Spoon the meat mixture into a small, wide-mouth thermos. Bag the cheese, tomatoes, lettuce, and sprouts in separate bags. Wrap the taco shells or pita pockets in a sandwich bag for assembling at lunch.

2 SERVINGS

VEGETARIAN TACO

1   tablespoon oil
¼   cup chopped scallions
1   small zucchini, diced
¼   green pepper, chopped
¼   cup sliced fresh mushrooms
⅛   cup sunflower seeds
¼   cup taco sauce
1   cup grated Monterey jack or cheddar
     cheese
½   ripe avocado, diced
2   cups alfalfa sprouts
2   corn taco shells or pita pockets

Heat the oil and lightly brown the scallions, zucchini, green peppers, mushrooms, and sunflower seeds. Add the taco sauce and cook for about 4 minutes. Spoon the vegetable mixture into a small wide-mouth thermos. Bag the cheese, avocado, and sprouts in separate bags. Place the taco shells or pita pockets in a sandwich bag. At lunchtime, stuff the warm vegetables, then the cheese, then the avocado and sprouts in the taco shells or pita pockets.

2 SERVINGS

BEAN TACO

Refried beans, also known as Frijoles, are usually sautéed kidney or pinto beans that have been previously cooked. You can use leftovers or purchase cans of prepared refried beans.

2   taco shells or pita pockets
1   cup refried beans, heated
¼   cup shredded lettuce
¼   cup alfalfa sprouts
½   small onion, chopped
2   tablespoons taco sauce
Shredded cheese

Pack the taco shells or pita pockets separately. Place the heated refried beans in a thermos container. Mix the lettuce and alfalfa sprouts and pack in a bag. Place the onion, taco sauce, and shredded cheese in separate containers for assembling at lunch.

2 SERVINGS

SOME OLD FAVORITES WITH A NEW TWIST

Sometimes you can give a lift to a favorite sandwich filling simply by chopping the ingredients together instead of slicing and layering; or using an ingredient in a totally new way, like in a Shrimpwich (page 69). Add a spicy mustard, or a curried mayonnaise, or a favorite spice. A new twist here, a tang there, bring new zest to sandwich fare.

SEAWICH TACOS

1   cup shredded cabbage
5   ounces small shrimp or flaked fish
½   cup low-fat cottage cheese
2   tablespoons mayonnaise
4   teaspoons seafood cocktail sauce (or 3 teaspoons catsup and 1 teaspoon grated horseradish)
½   teaspoon curry powder
Dash vegetable salt or salt substitute
6   taco shells or pita pockets

Mix all ingredients except taco shells. Chill. Stuff into the taco shells or pita pockets when ready to eat.

6 SERVINGS

TWO HELPFUL HINTS

Sandwiches *can* be made up ahead of time and stored in the refrigerator. Place in an airtight container with moistened paper towels, damp tea towels, or waxed paper placed between sandwiches to insure freshness. A week's supply can be made, stored, and used as needed — even for after school nibblers.

For "skinnywiches," use a rolling pin to roll bread thin and firm (kids enjoy doing this). Spread on mustard or mayonnaise, layer on thin slices of sausage roll or chicken, roll up, and secure with a toothpick.

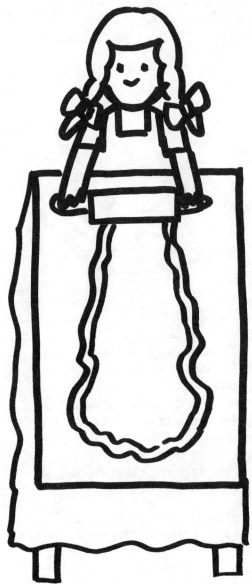

CORNED BEEF AND CHEESE SANDWICHES

1   cup grated cheddar cheese
½   cup ground cooked corned beef
¼   cup mustard
8   slices rye bread

Blend the cheese, corned beef and mustard ingredients, and spread on 4 slices of rye bread. Cover with the remaining 4 slices. Sandwiches may be brushed with melted butter and toasted before eating.

MAKES 4 WHOLE SANDWICHES

SHRIMPWICH

2   large romaine lettuce leaves
4   slices whole grain bread, lightly
        toasted
6   ounces cocktail shrimp in sauce
1   lemon wedge

Pack each ingredient separately. At mealtime, place the romaine leaves on 2 slices of bread and top with shrimp in sauce. Sprinkle with lemon juice. Top each with another slice of bread.

2 SERVINGS

GREEN WRAPPER SANDWICH

Separate, wash, and dry leaves of tender green cabbage, spinach, or romaine lettuce. Make a filling of ½ cup grated cheese, ½ cup finely chopped walnuts, and 2 tablespoons finely chopped celery. Combine with just enough yogurt or salad dressing to hold it together. Spread on the greens. Roll up and secure with a toothpick.

Variations: Stuff green wrappers with rice pilaf, chicken, fish, or cheese spreads.

1 CUP FILLING

MAKE-AHEAD CHICKEN SALAD ROLLS

4   hot dog rolls, partially split and toasted

Softened butter or margarine

1   cup finely diced cooked chicken *or* 2 (5-ounce) cans chunk chicken, well-drained

2   large ribs celery, diced

2   ounces Swiss cheese, finely diced

½   cup well-drained diced pineapple

¼   cup mayonnaise

Lightly spread the insides of the rolls with butter, covering to the edges. Set aside. Combine the chicken, celery, cheese, and pineapple. Stir in the mayonnaise, just to coat. Fill each roll with ½ cup of the chicken mixture. Wrap securely in foil, plastic bag, or freezer wrap. Store in the freezer. Remove as needed for packing lunches. Thaw in wrapper (takes about 3 hours). These sandwiches keep in the freezer for up to 2 months.

4 SERVINGS

KID PLEASERS
TACO MEATLOAF

1   **pound ground beef**
4   **ounces tomato sauce**
½   **package taco seasoning**
1   **egg, beaten**
½   **cup corn chips, crushed**
¼   **cup grated Monterey jack or cheddar cheese**

Mix all the ingredients, except cheese. Place in half-loaf size foil pans and top with cheese. Bake for approximately 1 hour at 325° F. until browned. When cooled, slice for sandwiches or freeze for later use. Kids love these.

4 SERVINGS

SPICY MUSTARD TO
ZIP UP A SANDWICH

¼   **cup mustard seeds**
⅓   **cup red wine vinegar**
¼   **cup water**
¼   **teaspoon ground allspice**
1   **garlic clove, crushed**
1⅓ **teaspoons vegetable salt or salt substitute**
1   **bay leaf, finely crumbled**

Combine the mustard seeds and vinegar in a bowl. Let stand for 3 hours. Place in a blender with the remaining ingredients and blend coarsely. Place in the top of a double boiler over simmering water. Cook for 5–10 minutes, until slightly thickened. Allow to cool. Put in a jar with lid and refrigerate.

MAKES ¾ TO 1 CUP

SARDINES ON TOAST

1 (3¾-ounce) can Norwegian sardines
    packed in tomato sauce
½ teaspoon dill weed
½ medium-size cucumber, thinly sliced
4 slices toast or 8 large rye crackers

Mash together the sardines (and sauce) and dill
weed. Pack in a container. Pack the cucumbers
and toast in separate plastic bags. When ready
to eat, spread the sardine mixture on the toast.
Top with the cucumber slices.

4 SERVINGS

TUNA AND WATERCRESS SANDWICH

1 teaspoon soy or corn oil margarine
3 teaspoons creamy low-cal cucumber
    dressing
2 slices wheat berry bread
½ cup packed watercress leaves
2 ounces tuna packed in water, drained
    and flaked

Combine the margarine with 1½ teaspoons of
the dressing and spread on one bread slice. Mix
the tuna with remaining cucumber dressing.
Layer on the watercress and the tuna mixture.
Top with the second slice of bread.

1 SERVING

CHICKEN ALMONDINE SANDWICHES

24 slices whole wheat bread
1 cup ground white chicken meat
¼ cup chopped blanched almonds
¼ cup mayonnaise or plain yogurt
Curry powder

Using a biscuit cutter or large cookie cutter, cut circles from each slice of bread. (Save the corers for bread crumbs.)

Blend the chicken and almonds. Moisten with mayonnaise or yogurt. Add a shake of curry powder. Spread on the circles of whole wheat bread. Garnish each circle with a small pimento strip. The perfect accompaniment for these sandwiches is green grapes—washed, dried, and bagged separately.

MAKES 24 OPEN-FACE SANDWICHES;
12 CLOSED SANDWICHES

SOME LIKE IT HOT!

If you're lucky enough to have a toaster oven or microwave in your office cafeteria or dining area, then these sandwiches make very practical and very good portables. Otherwise, save them for Saturday lunches when you'll want to treat everyone to something a little different from the rest of the week.

LIVERWURST KRAUT MELT

Spread one half of an onion roll with liverwurst. Top with green pepper rings. Moisten the sauerkraut with a drop of Italian dressing, (page 97), and pile on top of the peppers. Top with sliced Muenster cheese. Broil until the cheese melts. For a whole sandwich, warm the top slice of the bun in the toaster oven separately and add to sandwich before eating. In a microwave, heat on medium for 30–60 seconds, until the cheese is bubbly.

1 SERVING

MEATLOAF MELT

Into a loaf of Italian or French bread arrange slices of cold meatloaf. Spread with mustard or catsup. Place cheese strips on top. Wrap in foil and heat in a 350° F. oven for 10–15 minutes. In a microwave, heat on medium for 30–60 seconds until the bread is warmed and the cheese begins to melt. Cut into sandwiches and serve hot.

MAKES 10 TO 12 SANDWICHES

CORNED BEEF BURGERS

½   **cup ground cooked corned beef**
¾   **cup Russian dressing**
1   **small onion, chopped**
⅓   **cup pickle relish**
Whole grain hamburger buns
4   **slices Swiss cheese**

Mix the corned beef, dressing, onion, and relish. Spread thickly on buns. Top with the cheese. Place in an insulated container. When it is time to eat, heat in the oven for 20 minutes at 350° F. These sandwiches can be prepared ahead, wrapped, dated, and frozen for up to two weeks.

4 SERVINGS

CHEESY CHILI ROLL

1 submarine sandwich roll
1 cup chili with beans
¼ cup peanut halves
3 sprigs parsley, minced
¼ cup grated cheddar cheese

Split the submarine bun in half lengthwise. Spread one half with chili, then layer on peanuts and parsley. Sprinkle with grated cheese and add the top of the bun. Place in 375° F. oven until cheese melts. (Cut into mini-rolls for pint-size munchers.) Pack in an insulated container. Take along tortilla chips or cherry tomatoes.

2 SERVINGS

HAM 'N CHEESE WICH

½ cup chopped ham
1 tablespoon finely chopped onion
1 tablespoon Dijon-style mustard
1 whole wheat English muffin
2 slices Swiss or Monterey jack cheese

In a small bowl, combine the ham, onion, and mustard. Split the muffins and place on a cookie sheet. Spoon about ¼ cup of the ham mixture onto center of each muffin half. Place a cheese slice over ham mixture. Bake at 375° F. for 10–15 minutes, until light brown. In a microwave, heat on medium for 4½ minutes until the filling is hot and cheese just begins to melt.

2 SERVINGS

SOUPS AND STEWS

Whether it's a steaming mug of garden vegetable soup or a chilled cup of smooth melon soup, one thing's for sure — soup is a relaxing pick-me-up, perfect for any day's portable lunch.

And it's so convenient. Most soups can be made well in advance, frozen in serving-size containers or ice cube trays, and there you have it — a refreshing, nourishing meal-to-go.

I like to freeze most of my smooth soups in ice cube trays, and then defrost a few cubes at a time. Place cubes in the microwave, and you are minutes away from a hot thermos for lunchtime. For cold soups, cubes of soup are even better; they defrost as the morning wears on, and at lunchtime you have perfectly chilled, perfectly delicious soup.

Do experiment. Basically, you can puree any of your leftover cooked vegetables in a blender or

food processor, add a favorite herb or spice, stir in enough liquid (broth, milk, or cream depending on your preference), and you have a very elegant soup. Send along a plastic bag with garnishes — chunks of fresh veggies, croutons, sunflower seeds, or raisins — and add an apple to the brown bag; you have a nutritious portable lunch once again. See how easy it is!

Other quick-and-easy soups involve starting up the soup pot. Start your broth with fresh meat bones, or chicken bones, or fish bones. Let this simmer with an onion, carrot, sprig of celery, and a bay leaf. As the liquid reduces, you can add more if you have time and reduce again (this makes a richer broth), or complete your soup now. Simply strain the broth (use cheese cloth if you have small chicken or fish bones). Then add whatever you have on hand — fresh vegetables, dry beans, uncooked meats or fish, then uncooked pastas. Add ingredients in a logical order; those that need to cook longer go in first. Lastly, add any leftover *cooked* foods — a bit of leftover stew, diced-up leftover ham, leftover pasta. The amount of liquid used in making your soup should be about half that of solid ingredients: 1 cup liquid to 2 cups of vegetables, etc.

Of course, what I like best about soups even beyond convenience and economy is the nutritional value. All those vegetables that get spurned at dinner can reappear in the soup pot and suddenly they're acceptable. And kids do love everything about soup — enlist their help in cooking, and it's guaranteed they'll eat every drop at lunchtime.

SOUPER IDEAS!

★ Keep a supply of alphabet pastas to toss into vegetable soup when the kids are helping.

★ Save the liquid from cooking vegetables (with all those valuable nutrients) to use when you make broth.

★ Keep a refrigerated plastic bag of fresh vegetable odds and ends to add to your soup pot.

★ Send along a dollup of plain yogurt (packed separately in rinsed-out, small, used yogurt containers) to add to pureed soups. Delicious!

★ Make your own croutons for garnishes using toasted stale bread, flavored with garlic powder if you wish.

★ Float fresh uncooked veggies in a bowl of steaming hot broth for a wonderful low-calorie treat. (Send veggies packed separately.) Add a touch of sherry if it's beef broth, and you've made a truly elegant lunch.

★ Add cooked meats and beans to hearty soups.

★ Add cooked potatoes to soup, stews, and chowders – a wonderful thickener.

★ Remember to think of fruits when soup's on the menu. Chilled fruit soups are especially refreshing on a hot summer's day.

For a quick fruit soup, add water or chicken broth to fruits and melons (1 cup liquid, 2 cups fruit), and simmer until fork tender. Blend in a food processor or blender with a handful of fresh dill, mint, chives, or parsley. Serve frosty cold.

★ Mix-ins – those nutritional extras bagged for fun and freshness – are perfect additions to soup lunches. Send along any variety of fresh vegetable chunks, nuts, chopped or sliced hard-boiled eggs, scallions, raisins, olives, dried apples, granola flakes, crushed crackers, and croutons.

★ Steam and freeze those end-of-the-season garden vegetables that don't quite measure up to your table standards; they'll be great in the winter stock pot.

★ Grow plenty of extra parsley (a natural diuretic, extremely rich in iron, potassium, and chlorophyll), and other favorite herbs for a yearlong soup-making supply.

★ For fat-free soup using chicken or beef stock, chill the stock overnight so the fat will rise to the top and congeal. Remove the congealed fat before reheating.

FRESH MUSHROOM SOUP

2 cups vegetable or beef broth
¼ teaspoon onion powder
1¼ cups sliced mushrooms
1 teaspoon minced parsley

In saucepan combine the broth, onion powder and mushrooms. Bring to boiling; then reduce heat, cover, and simmer for 10 minutes. Remove from heat. Sprinkle with parsley. Pour half of recipe into thermos. The remainder can be frozen.

2 SERVINGS

INSTANT CUCUMBER-YOGURT SOUP

1 medium-size cucumber, peeled
8 ounces plain yogurt
2 medium-size scallions with tops, thinly sliced
¼ teaspoon dried dill weed
¼ teaspoon curry powder
1 garlic clove, crushed
½ cup milk

Quarter the cucumber and discard the large seeds. Thinly slice the cucumber into a bowl. Stir in the yogurt, scallions, and seasonings. Add milk to the desired soup consistency. Stir, cover, and chill well. Add 1 minty ice cube (freeze fresh mint sprigs in ice cubes) to each wide-mouth thermos.

3 SERVINGS

CREAM OF WINTER SOUP

Use your favorite winter squash: butternut, acorn, buttercup, or banana.

2 cups peeled diced potatoes
1½ cups winter squash, cut in chunks
½ cup chopped celery
1 garlic clove, minced
2 tablespoons chopped parsley
1 teaspoon dry mustard
1 teaspoon grated lemon peel
⅛ teaspoon fresh pepper
1½ cups chicken broth

1½ cups milk
Sunflower seeds, toasted

In a stockpot, combine the first 9 ingredients. Bring to a boil; then reduce the heat and simmer for 20 minutes until vegetables are fork tender. Blend the soup mixture in a blender or food processor until smooth. Return to the stockpot. Add the milk and heat thoroughly, but do not boil. Pour into the thermos. Wrap sunflower seeds separately to be sprinkled on the soup when ready to eat.

8 SERVINGS

LENTIL FRANK SOUP

½ cup cooked lentils
2-ounce fat-free hot dog, cut in chunks
1 cup chicken broth
½ cup thinly sliced carrots

Combine the lentils, hot dog, broth, and carrots in saucepan. Bring to a simmer, cover, and cook for 20 minutes. Pour into a thermos. Pack rye crackers or bread separately.

1 SERVING

CREAMY BROCCOLI SOUP

1 small bunch of broccoli or 1
      (10½-ounce) package frozen broccoli
1–2 cups skim milk
½ teaspoon grated nutmeg
½ teaspoon vegetable salt or salt
      substitute

Steam the broccoli until fork tender. Place in food processor or blender and process until smooth. Add milk to the consistency desired. Season with nutmeg and vegetable salt. Pour into a thermos; send along seasoned croutons for mix-in.

4 SERVINGS

ZUCCHINI SOUP

1 medium-size onion, chopped
1 medium-size potato, thinly sliced
⅛ teaspoon lemon pepper
¼ teaspoon curry powder
3½ cups chicken or vegetable stock
1 pound zucchini, sliced
2 tablespoons chopped parsley
Pimento for garnish

In large saucepan, simmer the onion, potato, pepper, and curry in stock for 5 minutes. Add the zucchini, and simmer for 10 minutes. Add the parsley, and simmer for 5 minutes. Process half the mixture in a blender or food processor until creamy. Return to the saucepan. Simmer for 1 minute. Serve hot or cold. This soup freezes well.

6 SERVINGS

SHAPE-UP SOUP

2   cups chicken broth
3   medium-size potatoes, peeled and diced
2   scallions, sliced
2   large carrots, diced
1   cup plain low-fat yogurt
1   teaspoon garlic powder

Combine the chicken broth, potatoes, scallions and carrots in a saucepan. Bring to a boil, cover, and simmer until the potatoes and carrots are fork tender. Pour half the soup into a blender or food processor and process until smooth. Set aside. Process the remaining soup mixture with the yogurt and garlic powder. Add to rest of mixture, stirring to mix well. This soup can be served cold or hot. Do not reheat after adding the yogurt. Pack a scallion or carrot stick for a stirrer. For thinner soup, add additional chicken broth or water.

6 SERVINGS

TOMATO ORANGE SOUP

4   large ripe tomatoes, chopped
4   carrots, thinly sliced
1   medium-size onion, sliced
2   garlic cloves, crushed
3   cups chicken broth

1   cup orange juice
1   teaspoon vegetable salt or salt substitute
6–8 sprigs parsley, chopped

Put first 5 ingredients in large soup pot. Bring to a boil, cover, and simmer for 25 minutes until the vegetables are fork tender. Place in blender and process until you have a desired consistency—chunky or smooth. Add the orange juice and vegetable salt. Sprinkle on chopped parsley. Chill. Send along fresh vegetable chunks, chopped hard-boiled eggs, croutons, or olives for mix-ins.

6 SERVINGS

ICED MELON SOUP

1   medium-ripe cantaloupe or small
    honeydew melon
1   cup chicken broth or apple cider
2–3 teaspoons lime or lemon juice
Dash vegetable salt or salt substitute
Dash freshly ground pepper
½   pound prosciutto, thinly sliced
    (optional)

Scoop out the melon and puree in a blender or
food processor. (There should be about 2 cups
of puree.) Add the chicken broth, lime juice,
and seasonings. Finely chop all but 2 or 3 slices
of prosciutto, and add to soup. Chill. Cut the remaining 2 or 3 slices of prosciutto into thin
strips for the top of the soup.

Variation: Omit the prosciutto and garnish
with fresh mint or a thin slice of lime.

3 SERVINGS

GAZPACHO

1 cup canned tomatoes, undrained
1 cup peeled and chopped cucumbers
¼ cup chopped green peppers
½ garlic clove, minced
1 tablespoon red wine vinegar
Dash onion powder
1 drop hot pepper sauce (optional)

¼ pound mushrooms, sliced
¾ cup tomato juice
Parsley and celery leaves

Combine the first 7 ingredients in blender or food processor and process until smooth. Stir in the mushrooms and tomato juice. Place in covered container in the refrigerator overnight. Pour into a thermos and garnish with chopped parsley and celery leaves. Send along any mixins you have on hand–croutons, olives, hardboiled eggs, nuts, and veggie chunks are especially good.

3 SERVINGS

NEW ORLEANS CHOWDER

2 (6½-ounce) cans minced clams, with liquid
1 (28-ounce) can whole tomatoes, undrained and chopped
2 cups water
1 large potato, peeled and cubed
2 medium-size onions, thinly sliced
1 medium-size green pepper, chopped
2 garlic cloves, minced
1 bay leaf
1 teaspoon vegetable salt or salt substitute
½ teaspoon dried basil
⅛ teaspoon pepper
1 (10-ounce) package frozen cut okra
1 pound flounder or sole fillets, cut into bite-size pieces

Drain the clams, reserving the liquid. Set the clams aside. In a Dutch oven, combine the clam liquid with all the remaining ingredients, except the okra and fish. Bring to a boil. Cover, reduce the heat, and simmer for 15–20 minutes or until the potatoes are tender.

Stir in the okra, flounder, and clams; bring to a boil. Reduce the heat and simmer, uncovered, for 8 minutes or until fish flakes easily. Remove the bay leaf before ladling desired amount into a thermos. Cheesy garlic bread is a filling accompaniment.

5 SERVINGS

STEAMING VEGETABLE CHOWDER

½ cup chopped onion
1 garlic clove, minced
1 cup sliced celery
¾ cup sliced carrots
1 cup cubed potatoes
3½ cups chicken broth

1 (17-ounce) can whole kernel corn,
    drained
¼ cup butter or margarine
¼ cup unbleached flour
2 cups milk
1 tablespoon prepared mustard
¼ teaspoon white pepper
⅛ teaspoon paprika
2 tablespoons diced pimento
2 cups grated cheddar cheese

Combine the first 6 ingredients in a large Dutch oven; bring to a boil. Cover, reduce the heat, and simmer for 15–20 minutes or until the potatoes are tender. Stir in the corn and remove from the heat.

Melt the butter in a heavy saucepan over low heat. Sprinkle the flour on top of butter, and stir until smooth. Cook for 1 minute, stirring constantly. Gradually add the milk, stirring constantly to prevent lumps, and cook over medium heat until bubbly and thick. Stir in the remaining ingredients and cook until the cheese melts, stirring constantly. Gradually stir the cheese mixture into vegetable mixture. Cook slowly until thoroughly heated. Spoon into insulated containers. This soup can be made up in advance and frozen.

5 SERVINGS

NEW ENGLAND CLAM CHOWDER

⅓   stick butter or margarine
2   large yellow onions, diced (about 3 cups)
2   celery ribs, chopped (about 1 cup)
¼   cup unbleached flour
¾   teaspoon vegetable salt or salt substitute
¼   teaspoon dried thyme or ½ teaspoon seafood seasoning
4   potatoes, peeled and diced
1   (8-ounce) bottle clam juice
6   cups milk
2   (8-ounce) cans minced clams, drained
2   teaspoons chopped parsley
½   teaspoon Worcestershire sauce

In a 4–6-quart kettle, melt the butter and sauté onion and celery until transparent, but not brown (about 3 minutes). Remove from the heat; add the flour, salt, and thyme; and stir until the vegetables are evenly coated. Return the kettle to heat.

Add the potatoes, clam juice, and just enough water to barely cover. Bring to a boil, lower the heat, and cover. Simmer for 15 minutes, or until the potatoes are almost tender.

Add the milk and bring just to boiling; lower the heat and add the clams. Stir in the parsley and Worcestershire. Ladle into a wide-mouth thermos. Pack chunks of cranberry bread separately.

8 SERVINGS

RAINY DAY SOUP

5   cups beef, vegetable, or turkey stock
2   cups shredded cabbage
½   pound low-fat frankfurters, sliced
1   cup diced tomatoes
½   cup uncooked small macaroni
1   medium-size onion, sliced
2   tablespoons grated parmesan cheese
½   medium-size garlic clove, minced
½   teaspoon caraway seeds

Combine all the ingredients in a large saucepan. Bring to a boil and reduce the heat. Simmer for about 30 minutes, stirring occasionally. Fill a thermos container and store the remainder in the freezer or refrigerator. Sesame bread sticks go well with this soup.

5 SERVINGS

QUICK VEGETABLE SOUP

1   small carrot, coarsely shredded
1   scallion, thinly sliced
2   medium-size mushrooms, thinly sliced
1   cup vegetable broth

Pack the vegetables in an airtight container. Place the hot broth in the thermos. At lunchtime, mix the vegetables and broth in a mug or bowl. Stir to blend. This soup is good for calorie counters also.

1 SERVING

BISQUE IN A HURRY

2   (10¾ ounce) cans condensed cream of shrimp soup
1½ cups skim milk
2   tablespoons dry sherry
6   hard-boiled eggs, chopped
Fresh chives, snipped
Nutmeg

Heat together the cream of shrimp soup and milk. Add more milk if the soup is too thick. Stir in the sherry. Pack the hard-boiled eggs in a separate container for adding to the bisque when ready to eat. Pour the soup into a wide-mouth thermos. Garnish with chives and dash of nutmeg.

4 SERVINGS

HOBO STEW

2   tablespoons olive or vegetable oil
2   tablespoons butter or margarine
1   large red or sweet onion, thick sliced
2   garlic cloves, finely minced
3   medium-size zucchini, cut into ½-inch rounds
1   green pepper, seeded and cut into thin strips
3   small tomatoes, peeled and quartered
1   (16-ounce) can chick-peas, drained

Heat the oil and butter in a large skillet over medium heat. Add the onions and sauté for 3–5 minutes. Add the garlic, zucchini, and green pepper and cook until slightly browned. Stir in the tomatoes and chick-peas. Cover the skillet and simmer slowly for about 20 minutes. Spoon into a wide-mouth thermos to serve over Chinese noodles or spooned into a pita pocket.

4 SERVINGS

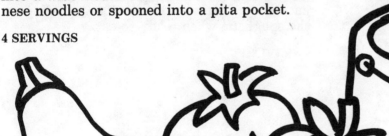

SPAGHETTI VEGETABLE STEW

1   **pound uncooked thin spaghetti**
3   **tablespoons butter or vegetable oil**
½   **cup chopped celery**
1   **cup chopped scallions**
1   **cup diced cooked ham (or other leftover meat)**
1½ **cups green peas, drained**
1   **cup plain yogurt**
Grated parmesan cheese

Cook the spaghetti according to the package directions and drain, or use leftover spaghetti. Heat the butter or oil in large skillet over medium heat, and sauté celery and scallions until transparent. Add the ham and peas and cook slowly until heated. Remove from the heat and add the yogurt. Mix well and pour over the spaghetti. Ladle into wide-mouth thermos and pack some parmesan cheese for sprinkling on the spaghetti when ready to eat.

4 SERVINGS

THE WILDEST CHILI

2 pounds ground beef
3 medium-size onions, chopped
1 small green pepper, chopped
2 garlic cloves, sliced
1 (28-ounce) can tomatoes
1 (6-ounce) can tomato paste
1 (4-ounce) can chopped green chilies
2–3 tablespoons chili powder
2 teaspoons cumin
2 teaspoons vegetable salt or salt
  substitute
2 (15-ounce) cans cooked red kidney
  beans, drained

In large soup pot over medium heat, cook the ground beef with the onions, green pepper, and garlic until the beef is browned and the meat juices evaporate. Add the tomatoes and their liquid, the tomato paste, and remaining ingredients, except beans. Heat to boiling. Reduce the heat to low; cover and simmer for 1½ hours, stirring occasionally. Add the beans; heat through. Pack in a wide-mouth thermos. Freeze extra in serving-size portions.

10 SERVINGS

MEX-TEX EGGS

12 ounces whole kernel corn
15 ounces tomato sauce
1 cup ripe olives, pitted
¼ cup thinly sliced scallions
1 tablespoon chili powder
½ teaspoon cumin
½ teaspoon caraway seeds (optional)
8 hard-boiled eggs, sliced in wedges
Corn chips

Place all ingredients except eggs and corn chips in a saucepan and simmer for 5–10 minutes. Fill a wide-mouth thermos with the mixture. Send egg wedges and corn chips separately. Add to the mixture before eating. Great.

4 SERVINGS

SALAD SENSE

Salads have come a long way from the old standard tossed (with lettuce, tomato, and cucumber) or the stand-bys of tuna and egg salads. And what a welcome step in the right direction! The popular salad bars in restaurants everywhere have taught us a lot – salads can be as creative as you like, as fattening or slimming as you build them. Best of all, salads can now hold their own as the main part of a meal.

KEEP PORTABLE SALADS FRESH!

My simple solution to keeping vegetable salads fresh for portable lunches is to pack each vegetable and mix-in in a separate plastic sandwich bag. The shredded lettuce, quartered tomatoes, sliced mushrooms, chopped eggs, raisins, etc., each have their own bag. Tuck all of the bags in a small plastic serving bowl (1-quart sherbet container will do) with lid and there's your salad (with bowl) to go. Be sure to send along the salad dressing in a separate container. I usually pack a frozen container of fruit juice (also in a baggie) on salad days to keep everything nice and crispy. You'll find that kids especially love putting together their own salads this way.

For toting premixed salads, such as Tuna-Pineapple Health Salad (page 100), or Confetti Macaroni Salad (page 109) a wide-mouth thermos works best. A wide-mouth thermos is such a good investment for soups, salads, and main dishes that I think it's worth investing in one for each brown bagger in your household.

Be sure to send along appropriate utensils for eating or tossing, and if possible, a paper or plastic plate to spoon the salad onto ... it really is nicer than eating out of the thermos.

ARE SALADS REALLY SLIMMING?

Of course, salads can be slimming, filling, and nutritious; but as with everything to do with weight control, you have to be prudent about what you choose and how much you consume. My best advice is to check some of the calories of the salad items you're not sure about, and remember that just because it's in a salad doesn't make it skinny. For example: ½ cup of either green or wax beans equals 25 calories; ½ cup kidney beans equals 108 calories; ½ cup chickpeas equals 360 calories. Need I say more!

Also leave room for plenty of lettuce and other salad greens. An entire 1½ pound iceburg lettuce has a mere 65 calories. Pile it on high. And don't forget spinach when you think of salad greens. Go easy on the dressing. Every extra tablespoon equals at least 100 additional calories. Even commercial low-calorie dressings are fairly high in calories. It's a good idea to *measure* 1 tablespoon, so you'll see exactly how much (or how little) that is. Try adding fresh herbs, wine vinegar, herb vinegars, or fresh lemon to your salads instead of dressings.

WHAT ABOUT SALT?

Many of us tend to reach for the salt shaker when we see salad. I make up a vegetable salt (page 33) and send it in a portable plastic salt shaker. It's a real flavor-enhancer, without all that unnecessary sodium.

SALAD DRESSINGS

TANGY TOFU DRESSING

1   cake tofu, cubed
1   cup plain yogurt
2   tablespoons toasted sesame seeds
1   tablespoon low-sodium soy sauce
1   tablespoon cider vinegar

Place all the ingredients in blender or food processor and process until smooth. Store in the refrigerator.

MAKES 2 CUPS

YOGURT ORANGE DRESSING

½   cup plain yogurt
2   tablespoons orange juice (concentrate)
1   tablespoon mayonnaise
⅛   teaspoon paprika
⅛   teaspoon celery seed

Mix the yogurt, orange juice, mayonnaise, paprika, and celery seed thoroughly. Refrigerate.

MAKE 1½ CUPS

TOSS-UP DRESSING

¼ cup sald oil
3 tablespoons vinegar
½ teaspoon herbal seasoning
¼ teaspoon dried oregano, crushed

Place all the ingredients in a jar and shake well until combined.

MAKES ABOUT ½ CUP

ZESTY TOMATO TOPPER

1 cup tomato sauce
2 tablespoons tarragon vinegar
1 teaspoon low-sodium soy sauce
½ teaspoon vegetable salt or salt substitute
½ teaspoon dried dill weed
½ teaspoon dried basil, crushed
½ teaspoon orange juice

Combine all the ingredients in a jar, cover, and shake. Chill thoroughly. Shake before topping salads.

MAKES 1 CUP

ITALIAN DRESSING

1 cup salad oil
¼ cup lemon juice
2½ cups wine vinegar
¼ teaspoon vegetable salt or salt substitute
½ teaspoon sweetener (optional)
½ teaspoon dried oregano
½ teaspoon dry mustard
½ teaspoon onion powder
½ teaspoon paprika
⅛ teaspoon dried thyme
1 teaspoon garlic powder or
1 garlic clove, minced

Shake all ingredients in tightly covered jar. Refrigerate at least 2 hours to blend the flavors. Shake before serving.

MAKES 3½ CUPS

LOW-CALORIE SALAD DRESSINGS

SLIM-TIME DRESSING

8 ounces tomato juice
2 tablespoons red wine vinegar
1 garlic clove, crushed
1 tablespoon chopped fresh parsley
1 tablespoon chopped fresh or frozen
    chives
¼ teaspoon Dijon-style mustard
Dash celery powder

Place all the ingredients in a jar and shake well.

3 SERVINGS

YOGURT LEMON DRESSING

½ cup uncreamed or dry curd cottage
    cheese
2 tablespoons lemon juice
½ cup plain yogurt

Combine all the ingredients in a food processor or blender and process until creamy. Store in the refrigerator.

MAKES 1 CUP

PINK ANGEL DRESSING

½ cup low-fat cottage cheese
¼ cup buttermilk
½ medium-size tomato, peeled, seeded,
    and chopped
¼ teaspoon celery powder
¼ teaspoon dried tarragon

In a blender or food processor combine the cottage cheese and buttermilk and process until smooth. Add the remaining ingredients and blend until creamy. Store in the refrigerator in covered jar.

MAKES ABOUT 1 CUP

BULGE-FREE SALAD DRESSING

1 cup unsalted tomato juice
1 cup red wine vinegar
1 teaspoon dried dill week
⅓ teaspoon dried chervil
⅓ teaspoon dried basil
1 teaspoon dried oregano
Pinch garlic powder
1 pint buttermilk

Combine the tomato juice, vinegar, and seasonings. Let stand in the refrigerator overnight. Add the buttermilk to the liquid. Keep refrigerated.

MAKES 3 CUPS

TAKE-IT-OFF DRESSING

2 tablespoons cider or wine vinegar
½ cup tomato juice
1 teaspoon onion, grated
Favorite seasonings such as parsley, horseradish, basil, oregano, or curry

Combine all ingredients in a jar and shake. This dressing has almost no calories—use freely and enjoy. Store in refrigerator.

MAKES ABOUT ½ CUP

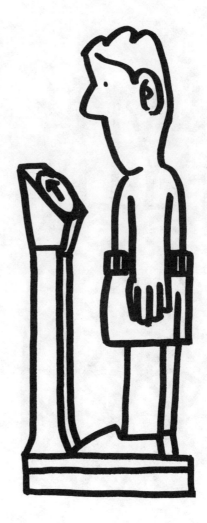

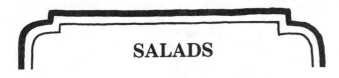

SALADS

TUNA-PINEAPPLE HEALTH SALAD

2   large pineapples or two large cans chunk pineapple, packed in its own juice
2   (7-ounce) cans tuna packed in water, drained
1   small carrot, pared and sliced
½   small green pepper, seeded and diced
½   small red onion, diced
1   tablespoon chopped fresh parsley
3   tablespoons cider or tarragon vinegar
Crushed nuts or sunflower seeds

If you are using canned pineapple, drain and reserve the juice for another use. Toss together all the ingredients, except the nuts or seeds. Chill and pack in wide-mouth thermos or plastic container. Send along crushed nuts or sunflower seeds for topping.

For a picnic or lunchtime surprise for your office mates, use fresh pineapple. Cut the pineapple in half lengthwise from bottom through the leafy crown. Cut out the fruit by cutting close to the rind, leaving a ½-inch-thick shell. Remove the hard core from each half of fruit; cut the remaining fruit into bite-size pieces. In large bowl, toss together all the ingredients, except the nuts or seeds. At lunchtime, mound the mixture into the pineapple shells. Serve on a pretty plate or in a bright basket. Bring along crushed nuts, sunflower seeds, raisins, and/or grated coconut to sprinkle on top.

4 SERVINGS

SOMETHING SPECIAL SALAD

1   head romaine lettuce
1   head iceberg lettuce
2   carrots
2   zucchini
¼   pound green beans
4–5 small artichoke hearts, cooked and
      drained
1   cup cherry tomatoes
½   cup ripe olives
2–3 hard-boiled eggs

Core, rinse, and drain the lettuce. Chill. Scrub the carrots and zucchini and cut into thin sticks. Cook the washed green beans in boiling water long enough to turn bright green, but still be crunchy. Drain and chill. Combine all ingredients, except the eggs, which should be packed separately. Pack your favorite dressing and some bread sticks, too.

4 TO 6 SERVINGS

ZUCCHINI/POTATO SALAD

½   cup water
¼   cup French or Italian dressing (page 97)
4   cups cooked sliced potatoes
1   medium-size zucchini, sliced thin
3   tablespoons thinly sliced scallions
½   teaspoon vegetable salt or salt
      substitute
1   cup low-fat cottage cheese
½   cup plain low-fat yogurt

Combine the water and salad dressing in wok or skillet. Add the potatoes to heat, about 5 minutes. Remove from heat and cool slightly. Place the potatoes and remaining liquid into a chilled bowl. Add the zucchini, scallions, and salt. Toss to mix. Cover and chill overnight. Before packing for lunch, mix in the cottage cheese and yogurt. Spoon into a wide-mouth thermos. Garnish with fresh dill sprig or mint if available.

6 SERVINGS

ON-THE-GO VEGGIES

3　cups grated cabbage
1　cup grated carrots
⅓　cup chopped onion
1　teaspoon poppy seed
2　tablespoons salad oil
2　tablespoons cider vinegar
1　teaspoon vegetable salt or salt
　　　substitute
2　green peppers, split lengthwise and
　　　seeded

In a medium-size bowl, combine the cabbage, carrots, onion, and poppy seeds. Toss lightly. Combine the oil and vinegar, shake until well mixed, and pour over vegetable mixture. Toss again and spoon into pepper halves. Wrap individually and refrigerate until ready to pack. Send along raisins, sunflower seeds, and cheese strips for toppings.

4 SERVINGS

MARINATED VEGETABLE SALAD

2　cups vinegar
¼　cup honey
1　teaspoon celery seeds
1　teaspoon dry mustard
½　teaspoon vegetable salt or salt
　　　substitute
2　pounds sliced cucumber
1　large sliced onion
2　pounds sliced carrots
2　pounds sliced green peppers

Mix first 5 ingredients together in double boiler and heat slightly until blended. Pour over vegetables. Mix well. Cover and refrigerate overnight. Serve on a bed of salad greens and send along some crunchy tacos, too. This colorful vegetable medley improves with age. Keeps well for a week or 10 days.

8 SERVINGS

SPAGHETTI TOSS-UP

4–6 dark green lettuce leaves
¼ medium-size cucumber, thinly sliced
4 ounces cooked chicken or turkey, cut
  in strips
1 cup cooked plain spaghetti, macaroni,
  or other pasta
1 small tomato, cut in wedges

Tear the dried lettuce into bite-size pieces. Toss
with thinly sliced cucumber, sliced chicken,
spaghetti or macaroni, and tomato wedges.
Pack the cold salad in a wide-mouth thermos.
At mealtime, spoon on your favorite dressing,
and lightly mix before eating. Garlic-flavored
croutons make a nice garnish.

2 SERVINGS

PACKABLE PEPPERS

1 cup ricotta cheese
½ cup grated carrots
1 teaspoon dried basil
1 teaspoon Dijon-style mustard
¼ cup finely chopped onion
2 bell peppers, halved and seeded

Combine all the ingredients except the peppers.
Stuff into the hollow peppers. Wrap and refrigerate until ready to pack.

4 SERVINGS

POTATO AND APPLE SALAD

3   medium-size potatoes
1   small apple, pared, cored, and diced
¼   cup chopped celery
1   hard-boiled egg, peeled and chopped
2   tablespoons chopped scallions
¼   cup plain yogurt
¼   cup mayonnaise
1   tablespoon chopped dill weed
¼   teaspoon vegetable salt or salt
      substitute

Cook the potatoes with the skins on in boiling water until tender. Drain. Peel and cut into ½-inch chunks. Mix the potatoes, apple, celery, egg, and scallions. Blend the yogurt, mayonnaise, dill, and vegetable salt and gently mix with the potatoes to coat well. Chill and pack in a wide-mouth thermos. Garnish the salad with a wedge of unpeeled apple or chopped walnuts.

4 SERVINGS

ITALIAN BEAN SALAD

1   (20-ounce) can chick-peas, drained, or 1
      (20-ounce) can green or yellow beans
1   (16-ounce) can red kidney beans,
      drained
1   cup sliced celery
½   cup sliced scallions
2   pimentos, diced
¼   cup salad oil
3   tablespoons cider vinegar
½   teaspoon dried oregano, crushed
½   teaspoon vegetable salt or salt
      substitute
¼   teaspoon pepper
Pita bread
3   hard-boiled eggs

Combine the first 5 ingredients in a large bowl. Place the oil, vinegar, and seasonings in a jar with a tight lid and shake well to mix. Drizzle over bean mixture. Toss lightly. Cover and chill several hours to season. Place salad in a wide-mouth thermos until time to eat. Scoop into pita bread and layer on separately packed egg wedges.

8 SERVINGS

SAILOR'S SALAD

1 package fresh spinach
2 (7-ounce) cans tuna packed in water, drained
1 small jar sliced pimentos
1 (6-ounce) can pitted large green olives
1 small jar marinated artichoke hearts
2 cups diced cooked potatoes
1 cucumber, peeled and thinly sliced
3 tomatoes, quartered
3 scallions with green tops, thinly sliced

Wash the spinach carefully and drain thoroughly. Combine the tuna, tomatoes, olives, potatoes, cucumbers, artichoke hearts, pimentos, and onions. Pack the mixture in a wide-mouth thermos; pack the spinach and your favorite dressing separately. Italian dressing (page 97) goes well with this salad.

10 SERVINGS

SUNSHINE SPINACH SALAD

2–3 cups fresh spinach pieces
1 orange
¼ cup sliced red onion
**Yogurt Orange Dressing (page 96) or
Italian dressing (page 97)**

Bunch the spinach and cut crosswise into 1-inch pieces. Remove the orange skin by cutting off in a spiral from the top of orange to bottom. Slice the orange crosswise into ¼-inch circles; cut the circles in half. Cut thin cross-wise slices from an onion and cut in quarters to measure ¼ cup. Place half the spinach in each of 2 individual wide-mouth thermos containers. Top with orange circles and onion slices. Send along the dressing in a separate container.

2 SERVINGS

EGGS-TRA SALAD

½ cup chopped scallions
½ cup sliced celery
½ cup Slim-Time Dressing
1 (10-ounce) package frozen green peas, cooked and drained
8 hard-boiled eggs, chopped
Lettuce and cherry tomatoes

Mix the scallions and celery with the dressing. Stir in the peas and eggs carefully. Chill in the refrigerator. Pack in a wide-mouth thermos with separate packages of green lettuce cups and cherry tomatoes for garnishing. A few melba toast crackers give some crunch to this lunch.

8 SERVINGS

WESTERN BEAN SALAD

1 pound cut green beans, cooked and drained
1 pound red kidney beans, cooked and drained
¼ cup chopped onion
½ cup Italian Dressing
1–2 teaspoons chili powder
½ teaspoon vegetable salt or salt substitute
1 cup sliced ripe olives
1 small green pepper, chopped
Mixed salad greens
Corn or tortilla chips

Combine the green beans, kidney beans, and onion in large bowl. Add the dressing, chili powder, and salt. Toss to coat well. Add the olives and green pepper. Toss to mix. Pack in a wide-mouth thermos. Place mixed greens and chips in separate bags. At mealtime, spoon the bean salad on the greens; use chips on the side.

6 SERVINGS

ROOSTER'S BEAK

4   ripe avocados, peeled and cubed
2   medium-size tomatoes, peeled and cubed
1   medium-size white or red onion, finely minced
2   garlic cloves, minced
2   tablespoons chopped fresh cilantro (also known as fresh coriander or Chinese parsley)
1–2 (hot) serrano chili peppers, finely chopped
3   tablespoons lemon juice
2   tablespoons olive oil
Salt and freshly ground pepper to taste

Combine all the ingredients and mix well. Cover and refrigerate 1–2 hours or overnight. Pack in a wide-mouth thermos.

8 SERVINGS

SHRIMP-CUCUMBER BOATS

1   cucumber
½   medium-size tomato, chopped
1   tablespoon chopped onion
3½ ounces baby shrimp, diced

Cut the cucumber in half lengthwise. With a spoon scoop out some of seed filling and mix with tomatoes, onions, and shrimp. Spoon the mixture back into the cucumber shells and wrap in foil securely. At lunchtime top the boat with 1 tablespoon Pink Angel Dressing (page 98). Send along some hard-boiled egg quarters for garnishes.

MAKES 2 BOATS

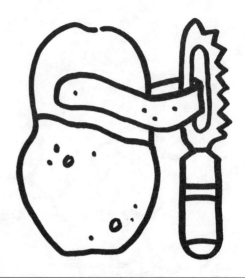

YOGURT POTATO SALAD

2   pounds small potatoes
1   cup plus 3 tablespoons plain yogurt
1¼ teaspoons vegetable salt or salt
     substitute
Dash cayenne pepper
4   scallions, finely chopped
½   tablespoon ground cumin

Boil the potatoes in their skins until just tender, Let them cool at least 2 hours. Peel and slice into ¼-inch rounds. Mix the remaining ingredients in a bowl and pour over potatoes. Mix gently, taste, and adjust seasoning. Refrigerate if not packing immediately. Pack some red and green pepper rings for colorful garnishes.

6 SERVINGS

CONFETTI MACARONI SALAD

1   cup cold cooked macaroni or rice
⅓   cup thinly cliced celery
3   tablespoons thinly sliced black olives
2   tablespoons chopped scallions
3–4 tablespoons Italian Dressing (page 97)
Vegetable salt or salt substitute
Lettuce, Spinach, or pita pockets

Combine the macaroni, celery, olives, and scallions. Toss with the salad dressing to coat. Season with vegetable salt to taste. Place in a wide-mouth thermos. Scoop onto lettuce or spinach leaves (packed separately), or into pita pockets.

2 SERVINGS

CUCUMBER SALAD

Mix 2 tablespoons fresh lemon juice, ½ teaspoon vegetable salt or salt substitute, ½ cup plain yogurt or buttermilk with 2 chopped cucumbers. Toss in some fresh dill or mint if you have some. Chill for 2 hours before serving.

4 SERVINGS

VERMONT FRUIT SALAD

2   cups plain yogurt
3   tablespoons maple syrup
½   teaspoon cinnamon
1   pound trail mix
3   large navel oranges, peeled and separated into sections
3   large bananas, peeled and sliced into ¼-inch rounds
3   large firm pears, quartered, cored, and sliced
2   pink grapefruits, peeled and separated into sections

Mix the yogurt, maple syrup, and cinnamon in a small bowl. Combine the remaining ingredients in a large mixing bowl. Pour the yogurt-syrup sauce over the fruit mixture and toss lightly. Cover and chill thoroughly. Spoon into a chilled wide-mouth thermos. This is sweet enough to use as a snack.

8 SERVINGS

SELF-CONTAINED MEALS-TO-GO

STUFFED SPUD SKINS, EGGS WITH EXTRAS, PACKED PIZZAS AND MORE

If you want to add a little variety, a dab of adventure, and admittedly, a bit more effort to your portable lunches, here are some perfect take-out ideas. What's extra special about these meals-to-go is that kids really love them because they are fun to eat, and they even have a kind of status attached to them. Who else gets to bring stuffed potato skins to school, not to mention pizzas or crunchy drumstricks?

Grown-ups will enjoy the fun of these foods, too, as well as the awareness that they carry plenty of nutrition, lots of versatility, and a heavy helping of flavor. Best of all, these self-contained meals can be filling without being fattening. You can, of course, stuff those spud skins or hard-boiled eggs with lots of calories, but you don't have to. You're in control of that situation, so pick and choose given your needs, and remember, you can pack flavor and nutrition without adding pounds. (A medium-size baked potato has only 90 calories, so don't blame the potato!)

Most of these foods can be made ahead, reheated while you have breakfast (if you have a microwave, it takes only minutes), wrapped tightly in aluminum foil, and packed in any sort of insulated container, such as a styrofoam container, a small insulated individual-size (they're advertised as being 6-pack size) carrier, a wide-mouth thermos, or even a small piece of old quilting. (I have a friend who keeps orphaned quilted mittens, pops a well-wrapped potato inside, and puts the whole thing in her brown bag!)

You really needn't pack much else with these meals as they are quite satisfying. Here's the perfect time to add a fresh in-season fruit to complete a perfect portable lunch.

STUFFED SPUDS

There's no limit to what you can put on or in potato skins, so keep in mind calories, nutrition, what will travel well, what will be better served warm (which is how these will be after a morning in the lunch box), rather than steaming hot (save those ideas for weekends or quick dinners).

Remember, too, that some people prefer *mix-ins*—potato scooped out and mixed-in with other ingredients before stuffing back into shell; others prefer *toppers*—additional ingredients are piled high on top of split potato. Mix-ins are nice because there are fewer containers to send along; toppers need to be packed separately.

POTATO TOPPERS AND MIX-INS

Here are some favorite toppers and mix-ins: grated cheese, chopped eggs, cottage cheese, tofu, yogurt, diced turkey, chicken cubes, vegetarian chili, sliced green onions, purple onion rings, toasted sunflower seeds, soy nuts, sesame seeds, peanuts, fresh parsley, chives, basil, cucumber cubes, sliced radishes, shredded carrots, marinated peas, broccoli and cauliflower, diced green peppers, croutons, tomato cubes, crushed taco shells, mung bean and alfalfa sprouts.

Have some leftovers, but not enough for a complete serving? Use leftover spaghetti sauce, scrambled eggs, chili, stew, tuna salad, cooked veggies (marinate if plain), or creamed veggies to heap on potatoes or to mix in.

SLIM-TIME POTATO

Bake the potato as usual. Split the potato and scoop out the inside and reserve for other uses. Bake the potato skins in a 350° F. oven for 15–20 minutes. Stuff with yogurt mixed with chopped cucumbers and radishes or serve the crunchy shells plain to go along with soup.

1 SERVING

CHEDDAR CHEESE AND CHUTNEY STUFFING

2   **cups grated sharp cheddar**
1   **stick butter or margarine, softened**
2   **tablespoons chopped scallions**
½   **cup chutney**

Mix the cheese and butter until creamy. Blend in the scallions and chutney. Pack in small covered containers for spooning over potatoes when ready to eat.

ENOUGH FOR 8 POTATOES

SPINACH AND COTTAGE CHEESE STUFFING

Steam a ten ounce package of fresh spinach until crisp tender, about 1½ minutes. Drain thoroughly and mix with ½ cup ricotta cheese or farmer cheese. Can be used as a low-calorie stuffing for scooped-out potato skins, or can be mixed in with the potato filling, and stuffed back in skins.

MAKES 1½ CUPS

CREAMED VEGETABLE TOPPING

1   cup finely diced fresh broccoli
1   cup chopped fresh asparagus
1   diced fresh zucchini
1   cup chicken broth
¾   cup heavy cream
1   cup fresh or frozen peas
Vegetable salt or salt substitute

Simmer the broccoli, asparagus, and zucchini in chicken broth for 2–3 minutes, until the vegetables are fork tender. Drain. (Save the broth to add to your soup stockpot.) Add the cream and peas to the vegetables and simmer a few minutes longer, until the cream coats the vegetables. Add vegetable salt to taste. Pack warm in a wide-mouth thermos for a potato topping.

ENOUGH TOPPING FOR 8 POTATOES

CHEESE-TUNA YOGURT STUFFING

1 (3¼-ounce) can tuna, drained and flaked
1 cup plain yogurt
1 hard-boiled egg, mashed
3 tablespoons pickle relish
¼ cup grated cheddar cheese
4–6 baked potatoes

Mix all the ingredients, except the potatoes and cheese. Partially scoop out the potato insides and replace with the tuna mixture. Sprinkle the cheese on top. Place in a toaster oven until the cheese melts. Pack in a wide-mouth thermos.

ENOUGH FOR 4 TO 6 POTATOES

POTATO BOATS

2 medium-size baking potatoes
¼ cup milk
2 teaspoons mustard
2 slices cheddar or other cheese
1 low-sodium or chicken frankfurter

Preheat the oven to 400° F. Scrub the potatoes and prick in several places with a fork. Bake for 1 hour or until tender. Remove the potato to a cutting board and cut a thin slice from the top of the potato. Scoop out the insides. Mash the potatoes; beat in the milk and mustard until the mixture is fluffy. Break the cheese into tiny pieces and stir into the potatoes. Refill the skins. Slice the frankfurter, and arrange on top of the potatoes. In the morning, bake 10–15 minutes at 350° F. until lightly browned, or reheat in a microwave for 2–3 minutes. Wrap in tinfoil and pack in a wide-mouth thermos.

2 SERVINGS

PACKED PIZZAS

QUICK PIZZAS

Spread toppings on slices of french bread, whole wheat English muffins, or stuff pita bread. Begin with 3 ounces of Pizza Sauce. (page 118). Then add any of the following toppings.

VEGETARIAN:
2 tablespoons chopped scallions, ½ cup grated sharp cheddar cheese, and ¼ cup thin sliced zucchini.

CHEESE:
½ cup grated provolone cheese and 1 tablespoon grated parmesan cheese.

MEXICAN:
½ teaspoon chili powder, ¼ cup Spanish sliced olives, and ½ cup grated Monterey jack cheese.

ITALIAN:
½ small sliced zucchini, ½ cup grated mozzarella cheese, ¼ cup sliced carrots, and 2 tablespoons sunflower seeds.

Broil until the cheese bubbles, about 5 minutes. Wrap in tinfoil and pack in insulated containers.

2 SERVINGS EACH

SIMPLE SIMON PIZZAS

1	pound ground beef
6	ounces tomato paste
½	cup water
¼	teaspoon dried oregano
⅛	teaspoon onion powder
6	whole wheat English muffins
8	ounces grated mozzarella cheese

In a skillet, brown the ground beef. Drain thoroughly. Add the tomato paste, water, oregano, and onion powder. Split the English muffins and toast. Spread the meat mixture over each muffin half. Top with cheese and toast until the cheese is melted. Wrap in tinfoil and pack in insulated containers.

6 SERVINGS

PIZZA SAUCE

2 tablespoons oil
½ cup chopped onion
2½ tablespoons chopped celery
2½ tablespoons chopped green pepper
1 cup chopped tomatoes
6 tablespoons tomato paste
1 teaspoon dried oregano
⅛ teaspoon dried sweet basil
½ teaspoon vegetable salt or salt
    substitute
¼ teaspoon dried rosemary

Heat the oil and sauté the onion, celery, and pepper until tender. Add the tomatoes, tomato paste, and seasoning. Cook slowly for about 30 minutes, stirring occassionally. Refrigerate and use as needed.

MAKES 2 SCANT CUPS

FAVORITE CRUSTLESS QUICHE

1 cup fresh green beans
1 cup sliced zucchini
6 carrots, diced
6 scallions with tops, chopped
6 ribs celery, diced
½ cup chopped fresh parsley
1 teaspoon vegetable salt or salt
    substitute
2 eggs, beaten
¼ cup skim milk
¼ cup ricotta cheese or low-fat cottage
    cheese
1 ounce parmesan cheese, grated
Dash nutmeg
1 tablespoon butter or margarine

Steam the greenbeans, zucchini, carrots, scallions, and celery separately until barely fork tender. Drain and mix with the remaining ingredients. Place in a lightly oiled shallow baking dish or non-stick quiche pan. Sprinkle with parmesan cheese. Bake at 400° F. for 10–15 minutes, until browned. Serve warm or cold. To tote, cut slices and reheat, then pack in an insulated container.

6 TO 8 SERVINGS

EGGS WITH EXTRAS

CHUTNEY-STUFFED EGGS

6   hard-boiled eggs
3   tablespoons mayonnaise
1   tablespoon finely chopped drained
    chutney
1   tablespoon finely chopped scallion
2   teaspoons curry powder
1   teaspoon Dijon-style mustard
½   teaspoon vegetable salt or salt
    substitute

Halve the eggs lengthwise; scoop out the yolks into a small bowl. Mash the yolks thoroughly. Stir in the mayonnaise, chutney, scallion, curry, mustard, and salt, blending well. Refill the whites with yolk mixture. Garnish with a small slice of green onion. Wrap tightly in plastic wrap. Makes a nice lunch with soup and whole wheat crackers.

6 SERVINGS

SUNNY EGGS

6   hard-boiled eggs
½   cup chopped scallion
½   cup chopped celery
½   cup plain low-fat yogurt or cottage
     cheese
1   tablespoon mustard
1   teaspoon curry powder (optional)

Halve the hard-boiled eggs, and scoop out the yolks. Combine the yolks with the remaining ingredients and stuff back into the egg whites. Sprinkle with paprika or use a thin slice of olive for a topper. Wrap in plastic wrap.

6 SERVINGS

POWER-PACKED EGGS

6   hard-boiled eggs
½   cup mayonnaise
1½ cups crab meat, tuna, or other flaked
     fish
¼   cup cottage cheese
1   teaspoon Dijon-style mustard

Halve the hard-boiled eggs and carefully remove the yolks. Mash the yolks. Combine with the remaining ingredients and mix well. Spoon into the egg white halves. Garnish with strip of pickle or thin radish slices. Wrap in plastic wrap.

6 SERVINGS

TUNA EGG BOATS

6   hard-boiled eggs
3–4 tablespoons mayonnaise
1   (3¼-ounce) can tuna, drained and
      flaked
1   teaspoon chili relish
1   teaspoon mustard
¼   teaspoon grated onion
Dash vegetable salt or salt substitute

Slice the eggs in half lengthwise and carefully remove the yolks. Mash the yolks and stir in the mayonnaise. Add the remaining ingredients, mixing well. Stuff into the egg whites. Sprinkle with a dash of paprika. Wrap individually in plastic wrap or pack several tightly in a plastic container.

6 SERVINGS

AND MORE ...

CRISPY OVEN-BAKED DRUMSTICKS

1   cup wheat, corn, or oat flake crumbs
⅓   cup wheat germ
⅓   cup grated parmesan cheese
⅓   cup almonds, chopped
½   teaspoon vegetable salt or salt
      substitute
⅓   cup butter or margarine
2   teaspoons grated lemon peel
16 chicken drumsticks, *peeled*

Combine the wheat crumbs with the wheat germ, cheese, almonds, and salt in plastic or paper bag. Melt the butter over low heat and stir in the lemon peel. Brush the drumsticks with the lemon butter, then shake, one at a time, in the crumb mixture. Place the drumsticks on a nonstick baking pan in a single layer. Bake in preheated 350° F. oven for 55–60 minutes until well done. Cool. To freeze, wrap each baked drumstick in plastic wrap. Place in airtight container to freeze. Will keep in the freezer for 2–3 weeks. Remove from freezer and place in refrigerator the night before packing for lunch.

**8 SERVINGS,
(2 DRUMSTICKS PER SERVING)**

EASY CRUNCHY DRUMSTICKS

⅓ cup plain dry breadcrumbs
2 tablespoons wheat germ
½ cup grated parmesan cheese
1 tablespoon dried parsley flakes
6 chicken drumsticks
4 tablespoons milk

Preheat the oven to 375° F. Mix the bread crumbs, wheat germ, cheese, and parsley flakes. Dip each drumstick in milk, then roll in breadcrumb mixture to coat evenly. Place on nonstick baking sheet and bake for 45–60 minutes, until the chicken is tender. When cool, wrap individually and freeze or keep in the refrigerator for 1 or 2 days. These are marvelous freeze-aheads to keep on hand.

6 SERVINGS

HAWAIIAN CHICKEN FINGERS

1 large chicken breast, skinned, boned, and split
1 tablespoon low-sodium soy sauce
1 tablespoon pineapple juice
1 small scallion, minced with some top
¼ teaspoon ginger

Combine all the ingredients in plastic bag and marinate for several hours, turning the bag occasionally. Remove the chicken, reserving liquid. Fry in nonstick pan or broil in oven, basting the chicken with the liquid marinade and turning the chicken once. When browned, remove from heat, and cool. Wrap in an airtight container.

2 SERVINGS

SARA'S NUTRITIONAL MEAL IN A BAR

⅓ cup butter or margarine
½ cup honey
½ cup molasses
1 egg
1¼ cups whole wheat flour
¼ cup dry milk
½ cup wheat germ
2 teaspoons baking powder
¼ teaspoon vegetable salt or salt
    substitute
½ teaspoon ginger
½ cup milk
1 cup rolled oats
1 cup nuts and sunflower seeds
1½ cups chopped raisins or dates

Cream together the butter, honey, molasses, and egg. Combine the flour, dry milk, wheat germ, baking powder, salt, and ginger. Mix well. Add the flour mixture alternately with the ½ cup milk to the butter/honey mixture. Stir in the oats, raisins, and half the nuts. Pour into a nonstick 8-inch by 8-inch baking pan. Sprinkle the remaining nuts on top. Bake in a preheated 350° F. oven for 30 minutes. Cool in the pan and cut into bars. Store covered in an airtight container. Freezes well.

MAKES 2 DOZEN

PACK A SNACK

Why pack between meal snacks if you want to cut down on calorie intake or you want to encourage kids to eat their lunches?

I think it's better to acknowledge that snacking and snack attacks are a way of life for most of us. Whether it's a midmorning coffee break at the office, snack time at school, getting overly hungry while waiting for a late business lunch, or having kids arriving home too ravenous to wait for dinner, there are bound to be several times a day when a well-planned snack is much better than grabbing the first available food (all too often a candy bar).

So I encourage you to send along a snack to be eaten "whenever." These snacks are nutritious, mostly in the lower-calorie category, and tempting. They are appropriate any time of day, pack easily, and go fine as something extra to have at lunchtime, too. As a matter of fact, I use many of these recipes as hors d'oeuvres and appetizers at dinner, as well as convenient packables for soup lunches.

Begin to think of snacks that give pleasure without pounds or sugar. They should be chewy or crunchy, energy-packed, and varied from day-to-day. Snack time is a perfect time to introduce new foods, too.

Keep plenty of plain yogurt in your refrigerator for a quick snack. Simply add fresh fruit, a teaspoon of honey, Grape Nuts™ cereal, raisins, or chopped nuts for a special sundae-like treat. Use fruits and vegetables creatively for snacking by stuffing or spreading with peanut butter, cheese spreads, or a mashed banana. Think of well-chilled fruit and vegetable juices at snacktime, too.

SNACKING SMARTS FOR KIDS OF ALL AGES

WALKING FRUIT SALAD

Slice an apple in half. Remove the core. Spread the cut sides with peanut butter. Sprinkle raisins, bananas, or nuts on top. Walk away and eat, or wrap in plastic wrap.

Variation: Using a medium-size whole apple, core the center, and stuff with peanut butter and any combination of raisins, bananas, and nuts.

1 SERVING

CHEESE ROLL

Carefully wash a cucumber or carrot. Peel and cut the cucumber lengthwise into quarters, or trim the ends from the carrot. Wrap a slice of Swiss or muenster cheese around the cucumber quarter or carrot and fasten with a toothpick. Use other cheeses if they will roll without breaking.

1 SERVING

STUFFED FRUIT

Wash a pear or an apple. Slice it in half through the core. Use a grapefruit spoon or measuring teaspoon to scoop out the core. Fill the space where the core was with cheddar cheese spread or peanut butter; put the halves back together.

1 SERVING

CRUNCH MUNCHKINS

Mix equal parts of raisins and peanuts. Pack in cups with lids. For fun, tie munchkins in a colorful cloth napkin.

PEANUT BUTTER CUPS

All ages enjoy a quick-energy snack. Make these ahead and keep on hand for bag stuffers and to tide famished teenagers over till lunchtime. Peanut butter cups are used by nutrition-wise teachers as a morning protein pick-up prepared by kids in the classroom.

1½ cups unsweetened granola cereal or
       Grape Nut Flakes™
1   cup non-fat dry milk
1   cup chunky or plain peanut butter
½   cup applesauce

Combine all the ingredients in a medium-size bowl and blend thoroughly. Place paper liners in eight 3-inch muffin cups. Spoon the mixture into the cups. Make up a day ahead.

Variations: Mix peanut butter with mashed bananas or orange juice, form into small balls, and roll in crushed peanuts, sesame seeds, wheat germ, grated coconut, raisins, chopped cashews, or chopped dried fruit. If you like, after rolling into balls, place on cookie sheet in the freezer until firm. The balls will store better and won't stick together.

8 SERVINGS

STUFFED STRAWBERRIES

1 **pint fresh strawberries**
2 **tablespoons crumbled blue cheese**
2 **tablespoons ricotta cheese**
Dash allspice

Clean and dry the strawberries, leaving the green caps on. Carefully slice the strawberries in half cross-wise. Blend the blue cheese, ricotta, and allspice until creamy. Spread the bottom half of the strawberry with the cheese spread. Top with second half. Pack in a wide-mouth thermos.

MAKES 18 TO 24 BERRIES

GO-WITH CELERY CHUNKS

6   celery ribs
½   cup pimento cream cheese
2   tablespoons chopped chives
1   tablespoon Dijon-style mustard
1   tablespoon dry sherry

Cut the celery ribs into 2-inch pieces. Combine the cheese, chives, mustard, and sherry. Stuff the mixture into celery chunks. Wrap in plastic wrap for travel; refrigerate extras for an after-school snack.

MAKES 24 CHUNKS

SKINNY DIP

½   cup plain yogurt
1½ cups ricotta cheese
6   tablespoons orange juice concentrate
Dash nutmeg

Place all the ingredients in a blender or food processor and process until creamy. Pack in a chilled container with lid. Pack separately wedges of fresh melon, pineapple, apple slices, grapes, or bananas for dipping.

MAKES 2½ CUPS

SLENDERELLA'S STIX

1   tablespoon low-sodium soy sauce
1   tablespoon grated parmesan cheese
1   package sesame sticks
2   cups Shredded Wheat™ bits
2   cups Cheerios™ cereal
2   cups plain popped corn
2   tablespoons roasted soybeans

Combine the soy sauce and parmesan and sprinkle over the remaining ingredients. Heat in 250° F. oven for 45 minutes, stirring often. Pack in plastic bags or cups.

4 TO 6 SERVINGS

TRIM-A-POUND CREAM CHEESE

Blend ½ cup low-fat cream cheese, ½ cup dry curd cottage cheese, and ½ cup plain yogurt. For variety add a shake of curry, garlic, or celery powder.

MAKES 1½ CUPS

GOLDEN CHEESE CORN

3   quarts freshly popped corn
½   cup grated cheese
¼   cup butter or margarine
¼   teaspoon vegetable salt or salt
     substitute
¼   teaspoon red pepper sauce

Preheat the oven to 300° F. Combine the popcorn and cheese in large baking pan. Set aside. In small saucepan over low heat, melt the butter or margarine. Add the salt and red pepper sauce. Cook 1 minute. Add to the popcorn, tossing lightly to mix well. Bake 15 minutes, until crisp. Store in a tightly covered container for up to 2 weeks.

MAKES 3 QUARTS

TOFU CHEESE DIP

1   cup diced tofu
½   cup low-fat milk
1   cup grated sharp cheddar cheese
½   cup grated Swiss cheese
2   tablespoons grated parmesan cheese
¼   teaspoon dry mustard
Apple slices
Cubes of whole grain bread

Place the tofu and milk in a blender and blend until thick and smooth. Transfer to the top of a double-boiler. Stir in the cheeses and mustard. Heat over simmering water until the cheeses are melted. Beat smooth with a wire whisk or return to the blender and blend a few seconds, until shiny and smooth. Place in a small covered insulated container and take along apple slices and bread cubes for dunking.

MAKES 2 CUPS

CRUNCHY CARROT BALLS

1   (3-ounce) package cream cheese, softened
½   cup grated cheddar cheese
1   cup grated carrots
⅓–½ cup Grape Nuts™ cereal
2   tablespoons finely minced parsley

Beat together the cream cheese and cheddar cheese until creamy. Stir in the grated carrot. Cover and chill for 30 minutes. Shape into small balls and roll in a mixture of cereal and parsley to coat. Store in an airtight container in refrigerator, and wrap individually in plastic wrap for travel.

MAKES 14 BALLS

PEANUT BUTTER DIP

½   cup peanut butter
¼   cup applesauce

Mix the peanut butter and applesauce until creamy. Pack fresh fruit slices separately to dip.

MAKES ¾ CUP

SUNFLOWER DIP

1½ cups sunflower seeds
1   cup walnuts
¼   cup peanut butter
½   teaspoon lemon juice
2   tablespoons mashed bananas

Place the sunflower seeds and walnuts in blender or food processor and process until finely ground. Mix in a bowl with the peanut butter, lemon juice, and bananas. Use as a dip or to stuff celery or zucchini sticks.

MAKES 1½ CUPS

PEANUTTY DIP

½ of a 6-ounce can frozen orange juice
    concentrate
1 cup creamy peanut butter
1 cup plain yogurt
Fresh fruit

Let the orange juice stand at room temperature
about 10 minutes. Combine the peanut butter
and yogurt. Stir in the juice until smooth and
creamy. Pack in small cups with lids. Send
along fresh apples, oranges, or grapefruit to
dip.

MAKES 2¼ CUPS

NUTTY BITES

1   small package cream cheese, softened
2-3 tablespoons chopped pecans or
    peanuts
6   slices raisin bread

Blend the cheese and nuts. Spread on the
bread. Cut into triangles.

MAKES 12 BITES

CHILI CON QUESO

1   pound cheddar cheese, cut into
    chunks
1   medium-size can tomatoes
4   ounces green chiles, seeded and
    chopped
1   large onion, finely chopped
Dash vegetable salt or salt substitute

Combine all the ingredients in the top of double
boiler. Break up tomatoes. Place over hot water, covered, until the cheese melts completely.
This spread is delicious on English muffins,
crackers, or as a dip for corn or nacho chips or
fresh veggies, or for stuffing eggs.

MAKES ABOUT 3 CUPS

TANGY TEX-MEX DIP

4   cups grated sharp cheddar cheese
2   cups cooked and mashed beans
        (white, limas, pinto, kidney or
        pink beans)
½–⅔ cup jalapeño relish
¼   cup chopped sweet red pepper
2   tablespoons chopped green olives
Chopped fresh parsley
Tortilla chips or fresh vegetables

Combine the cheese, beans, and relish in large bowl and beat well. Stir in the red pepper and olives. Cover and refrigerate for at least 1 hour. Spoon into individual 4-ounce containers with lids for packing. Sprinkle on the parsley. Bag up tortilla chips or fresh vegetables for dunking at lunch or snack time.

MAKES 7 CUPS

BEVERAGES

THE OVERLOOKED POWER PACKABLES

All too often we overlook beverages as nutritious energy sources. In a sense, our beverage-awareness hasn't kept up with our kitchen equipment. Most kitchens now have either a blender, food processor, or juicer, if not all three. So begin thinking of beverages as something more than orange juice in the morning, milk or soft drinks at lunch, and whatever is handy to quench your thirst.

Instead, consider beverages as easy-to-pack snacks, meals-in-one, energy-boosters, and probably the very best way to camouflage nutritional necessities for finicky eaters. Won't eat eggs? Toss one in a Blender smoothy (page 140) and no one will ever be the wiser (but all will be healthier!). Won't drink milk? Try a Kid-Pleaser Thirst Quencher (page 145) and the milk problem will be gone. Spurns fruit? Try a thick Berry Blend (page 147) and fruit becomes a frothy fruity delight.

Basically, all you have to do is plug in your blender or food processor, and create any combination of fresh peaches, plums, blueberries, strawberries, bananas, melons, apples, and oranges with milk, kefir, yogurt, or fruit juices. (Be sure store-bought frozen or canned juices say "unsweetened" or "no sugar added.") The ratio of fruit to liquid should be about 1 part fruit to 2 part liquid, depending on how thick you want your shake. A squeeze of lime juice or a sprig of mint adds plenty of zip.

For more power, add raw egg, peanut butter, wheat germ protein powder, or nutritional yeast.

Half the fun of making your own drinks is creating new and special taste treats. Most soft-fleshed fruits whip into a thick sauce-like frappe. To thin, dilute with a light splash of spring water or a spritz of sparkling water. Try cucumber coolers, a fresh tomato juice cocktail spiked with tangy herbs or spices, or a dash of Angostura bitters in a carrot-cucumber juice combo, a pinch of thyme in tomato-cabbage juice, or a pinch of nutmeg in apple-peach nectar.

And don't overlook the robust flavors of fresh-squeezed fruit and vegetable juices. They are wonderfully refreshing on hot summer days, and packed with the flavor and vitamin C we all crave on dreary winter days. Try juicing the whole fruit or vegetable to get the pulp, which contains minerals, fiber, and bioflavonoids.

If you or a household member tend to be an habitual meal-skipper—especially a breakfast skipper—these beverages should be viewed as necessities, rather than snacks or extras. They contain enough nutrition and energy to change your outlook on the whole day ahead.

BLENDER SMOOTHY

This makes an energy-meal-in-a-glass for anyone on the run.

1   **cup chilled skim milk**
½   **cup plain yogurt**
1   **medium-size banana**
¼   **cup pineapple kefir**
1   **egg (optional)**
Wheat germ

Combine the milk, yogurt, banana, kefir and egg in a blender and process until frothy. Sprinkle wheat germ on top.

1 SERVING

BANANA NUT SHAKE

1   **banana**
2   **tablespoons peanut butter**
¾   **cup low-fat milk**

Combine all the ingredients in a blender and process until smooth and creamy. Pour into a thermos. Include a spoon or a straw for sipping.

1 SERVING

PICK-ME-UP

1½ cups skim milk or fruit juice
2 teaspoons nutritional yeast
2–3 tablespoons protein powder
¼ cup plain yogurt
Fresh fruit (bananas, apples, strawberries, peaches, raspberries, or your choice)

Combine all ingredients in a blender or food processor and process until well blended. Pack in thermos and shake well before drinking.

Variation: Omit the fresh fruit and add 2 tablespoons carob powder and 3 tablespoons carob ice cream.

1 SERVING

TANGERINE TAKE-OFF

1 (6-ounce) can frozen tangerine juice concentrate
18 ounces cold water (3 juice cans) or sparkling water
½ cup apple cider

Combine all the ingredients and shake well. Pack in a cool thermos.

4 LARGE GLASSES

BANANA-ORANGE SHAKE

1   **ripe banana**
2   **tablespoons frozen orange juice
      concentrate**
½ **cup milk**
½ **cup plain yogurt**

In a blender or food processor, combine all the
ingredients and process until smooth. This is
good as a breakfast drink, or pack in a thermos
and shake well before drinking.

1 SERVING

NATURAL BUBBLY

½ **cup pineapple chunks**
½ **cucumber, chopped**
1   **teaspoon orange juice**
Ice cubes
½ **cup sparkling mineral water**
1   **pinch ginger**

Combine the pineapple, cucumber, orange juice
and few ice cubes in a blender. Process briefly.
Add the sparkling water and pinch of ginger.
Pack in a chilled thermos.

1 SERVING

VEGGIE APERITIF

3 large carrots, grated
2 celery ribs with leaves, chopped
1 tomato, peeled and chopped
½ cucumber, chopped
2 sprigs parsley, minced
¼ teaspoon vegetable salt or salt substitute
1 teaspoon lemon juice

Mix all ingredients in a blender or food processor until liquified. Add water if necessary. Serve with a half stalk of celery for a stirrer. This is a terrific appetizer for a dinner party— serve frosty and cool in summer, piping hot in winter. To take out, pour in a thermos.

4 SERVINGS

WATERMELON COOLER

Blend chunks of watermelon (with the rind removed) in a blender or food processor until slushy. To pack, pour in a chilled thermos.

1 SERVING

PIZZA TOMATO DRINK

Put 6 ounces of tomato juice in a blender. Add ⅛ teaspoon of oregano, ⅛ teaspoon of parsley, a dash of garlic powder, and a dash of vegetable salt. Whirl to blend and pour over ice cubes.

1 SERVING

PARTY PLEASER

1   **large can frozen lemonade**
      concentrate
2–3 cups water
½   **cup orange juice**
½   **cup apple juice**
Fresh orange or lime

Mix the lemonade with the water. Add the orange and apple juices. Slice fresh orange or lime for colorful floaters. Pack in a chilled thermos.

6 SERVINGS

APRICOT NOG

1 cup orange juice
½ cup skim milk
¼ teaspoon vanilla extract
2 cups apricot halves
1 medium-size banana

Place all ingredients in a blender or food processor and process until smooth. Chill thoroughly. Pour into a thermos. Tuck in a straw for cool sipping.

2 SERVINGS

KID-PLEASER THIRST QUENCHERS

Put a cup of milk, a sliced banana, and a couple of ice cubes into a blender. Turn the blender on high speed. In a few seconds, you'll have a creamy fruit frappe that not only tastes good, but is nutritious as well. Pour in a chilled thermos for a take-out treat.

1 SERVING

ORANGE FIZZ

1 (10-ounce) bottle sparkling water
1 quart orange juice

Mix and pour over crushed ice in a thermos container.

4 TO 6 SERVINGS

GRAPE SMOOTHIE

¼ cup grape juice
¾ cup pineapple juice
1 cup plain yogurt
1 ripe banana
2–4 ice cubes

Place all incredients in a blender and process until frothy. Pour into a thermos. Include a straw for added fun.

2 SERVINGS

TOFU SMOOTHIE

½   cup milk
½   cup diced tofu
2   medium-size bananas
1   cup orange juice
¼   cup carob powder or unsweetened
      cocoa

Place the tofu in a blender. Peel the bananas
and add to the blender with the orange juice
and carob powder. Blend on high speed until
frothy. Pack in a thermos.

4 SERVINGS

NUTTY MILK SHAKE

2   cups milk
1   frozen banana
½   teaspoon vanilla
¾   cup diced fresh fruit
1-2 tablespoons wheat germ
¼   cup nuts

Place all ingredients, except the nuts, in a
blender and process until frothy. Pour in a
chilled thermos. Pack the nuts in a bag for
sprinkling on top when ready to sip.

2 SERVINGS

BERRY BERRY

1 cup orange juice
1 egg
1 (10-ounce) package frozen strawberries
½ cup non-fat dry milk
½ cup water
1 tablespoon wheat germ

Place all the ingredients in a blender and process until smooth and frothy. Pour in a thermos, and shake well before drinking.

4 SERVINGS

BERRY BLEND

1 cup strawberries, raspberries, or
    blackberries
1 cup plain yogurt
1 cup skim milk

Whirl all ingredients in a blender until the berries are pureed. If you've used raspberries or blackberries, pour through a fine strainer to remove seeds. Pour in a thermos. Pack a colorful straw. Freeze extras.

3 SERVINGS

ALMOND MILK

Allergic to milk? Try this drink.

1   cup almonds
4   cups boiling water
6   pitted dates or 3 tablespoons raisins

Blanch the almonds by placing in boiling water. Turn off the flame, cover the pan, and allow the nuts to soak for 10 minutes. Remove the skins from almonds. Place the almonds in blender with 1 cup of the cooking water. Blend until the almonds are finely grated. Add the dates or raisins and gradually add the remaining water. Blend well. To thin, add more water or unsweetened fruit juice. Serve chilled.

MAKES 4 CUPS

PEANUT BUTTER SMOOTHIE

2   cups milk
½   cup non-fat dry milk
½   cup peanut butter
¼   cup orange juice concentrate

Combine the milk and dry milk in a blender and process until smooth. Add the peanut butter and orange concentrate and blend until well mixed and smooth. Drink slowly.

3 SERVINGS

CARROT NOG

½ cup thinly sliced carrots
1 can crushed pineapple
1 can orange juice
1 cup milk
½ cup whole cream

Place all the ingredients in blender and process until smooth and creamy. Pour in a thermos.

3 SERVINGS

FRUITY FROSTY

2 oranges
1 egg
1 cup milk
¼ cup strawberry kefir
¼ cup strawberry jam

Peel the oranges and cut into chunks. Place in a blender with the remaining ingredients. Blend until smooth. Pour into a thermos.

4 SERVINGS

NOT-TOO-SWEET SWEETS

As a food service director who has overseen the careful feeding of over 109 million individual meals, I *know* that dessert is the first food that kids look for on the lunch tray. And it doesn't take much unofficial sleuthing to conclude that adults are no different — that craving for sweets isn't something we tend to outgrow!

My approach, as a nutritionist, to the whole issue of sweets and the question "to have or have not" has been to work with the problem rather than to deny that it exists. The key to making some headway is education—education that begins right in the kitchen at an early age (but it's never too late). Basically, you want to clearly identify just how much sugar you consume in soda pop or ice cream, for example, and then explain what that sugar does to your body. Next, you want to show that the cravings for sweets can be satisfied in more healthful ways with appealing natural ingredients used in imaginative recipes.

So my advice is first to *educate*, and then *substitute* rather than *deprive* when it comes to sweets.

EDUCATE

First you can educate very young children by the example you set. Kids readily accept fresh fruit at school, if their parents have limited sweets for themselves and their children. Kids who haven't been limited are easy to spot. One fourth-grader, when seeing the fresh banana on the tray, asked, "Where's my dessert?"

Cut the sweet talk by teaching children some facts—that caffeine in soda pop and chocolate is a powerful nerve stimulant that causes increased heartbeat, insomnia, nervousness, restlessness, hyperactivity, and lack of concentration. Help older children make the connection between getting into discipline problems after a sugar-filled lunch, and feeling calmer when they haven't overdosed on sugar. Have kids measure the 3 teaspoons of sugar in 1 plain cookie , the 4 teaspoons in 4 ounces of ice cream, the 6 in a slice of apple pie, and the 9–10 in a 12-ounce soft drink. This experience is a real eye-opener. Then point out that to obtain from food the 38 grams of sugar found in one soft drink and a candy bar, one would have to eat four apples, four pears, and one banana.

Since tooth decay affects 95 percent of our children, dentists urge concerned parents to avoid foods or drinks that cling to the teeth, such as sticky, sugary sweets. But cola drinks are culprits, too. Cola drinks not only pack up to 46 milligrams of caffeine in a 12-ounce drink, plus sugar, artificial colors, and artificial flavorings, but they also cause an acid attack upon tooth enamel. The high phosphoric content of most soft drinks upsets the calcium, potassium, and magnesium balance in the body.

A vivid experiement you can do at home or in the classroom is to take a baby tooth that has just fallen out, let the children examine it carefully, and then place it in a glass with a cola drink. The children will never forget what happens over the next few days, as the tooth gets eaten away (often it splits in pieces) by the cola. A powerful visual lesson for us all!

The kitchen is the best learning center in the home. Involve kids in simple baking, which not only provides fun but a healthy sense of accomplishment while you are teaching good nutrition all the time.

Switching to healthful sweets means selecting recipes that contain nutritious ingredients. Use healthful trade-offs such as half-and-half flour (half whole wheat and half regular flour or oat flour which is rolled oats placed in the blender and pulverized), eggs, nuts, seeds, non-fat dry milk, and fresh and dried fruits.

Talk about your choice of ingredients, allow nibbling so children taste their natural sweetness, explain what you are substituting, as well as what you are adding. Take a favorite recipe and modify it with your kids, so they understand what you have done. The goal is not to "fool" anyone, but for everyone to realize that you *can* have your cake and eat it too!

NUTRITIONAL SWITCHING IS AS EASY AS 1, 2, 3 ...

Boosting the nutritional content of sweets is simple
mathematics—a little addition and subtraction.

Toss ¼ cup wheat germ (which is rich in B
vitamins) for every 1 cup flour into a basic
cookie recipe. Subtract 1 cup of chocolate
chips and add half a cup of raisins and half a
cup of carob chips.

Subtract white flour and replace it with equal
parts of wheat flour and unbleached flour.
Blenderize rolled wheat and oats to make
flour energy-packed with nutrients.

For fiber and crunch add sunflower seeds,
grated coconut, dried fruits, sesame seeds,
and rolled oats.

Get the idea? Here's some more specific recommendations.

Wheat Germ. The heart of the wheat kernel, wheat germ is an excellent source of protein, B-complex vitamins, vitamin E, and iron. It is a nutrient-booster to most any foods and can be gently folded into cookie batter with ease (¼ cup to 1 cup flour). Remember to keep wheat germ tightly covered and refrigerated because it contains a vegetable oil that can go rancid.

Raisins. Not only for oatmeal cookies, these nuggets of instant iron add chewiness to almost any cookie or pudding.

Nuts. Almost any nut will flavor cookie batters, but choose nuts that are unsalted. Add chopped peanuts to peanut butter cookies. Pecans add a sweeter flavor than English walnuts, so choose walnuts when making a sweeter cookie dough or for yogurt sweetness. Black walnuts add a flavor all their own and are delicious sprinkled in cookies or on fruit desserts. Nuts are excellent sources of B vitamins. Toast rolled oats lightly in the oven for an inexpensive nut stretcher. Roll nuts and dried fruit in flour before adding to cakes to keep them from settling to the bottom of the pan.

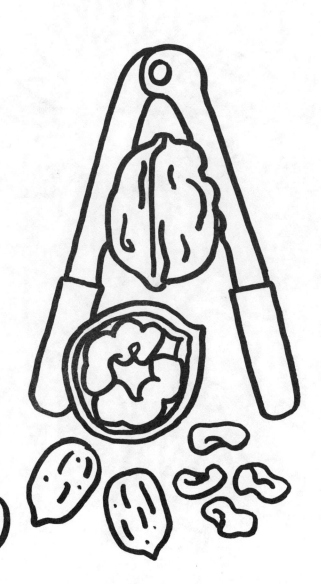

Dried Fruits. To spark flavor, add chopped, dried apricots or apples to cookie dough. They are fairly expensive, so let the fruits be the star attraction. Use as garnishes on frozen yogurt, too.

Coconut. Whether the cookie is filled with grated coconut, rolled in sweetened coconut, or sprinkled with toasted coconut, there is pleasure in store. Coconut adds interest and fiber to a cookie. Grate some on fruit desserts, puddings, and yogurt.

Sunflower and Sesame Seeds. Used with or instead of nuts, these seeds add flavor and crunchiness, as well as protein and calcium, to cookies and sweet breads.

Non-Fat Dry Milk Powder. Boost calcium, protein, and vitamins A and D by adding ¼ cup milk powder for every 1 cup of flour when baking. You can safely add 4 or 5 teaspoons of dry milk to any cookie recipe (without subtracting anything else).

Flour. Whole wheat flour can usually be substituted for a white flour in a recipe, cup for cup. If your family isn't ready for the hearty flavor of whole grains, you may wish to substitute Transition Flour for some of the white flour. Each time you bake, gradually increase the amount of Transition Flour until you have convinced your family to go whole grain.

Here's a time-saving recipe for a quantity of Transition Flour. To 5 pounds of unbleached flour, add 1 cup each of wheat germ, powdered milk, and soy flour. This nutritious flour mix can be used in any recipe calling for white flour.

Enjoy experimenting with a variety of grains —rye, oat flour, millet flour, and buckwheat flour.

Carob. Naturally sweet, with a flavor all its own, carob provides a healthy alternative to chocolate. Carob is naturally high in iron and fiber rich. Unlike chocolate, it contains no caffeine and is lower in fat (fat content of carob is 2 percent; fat content of chocolate is 52 percent). Switch to carob flour, powder, chips and nuggets. (Purchase chips and nuggets with no added sugar.)

To replace chocolate with carob powder, use 3 tablespoons carob powder plus 1 tablespoon water and 1 tablespoon vegetable oil to equal 1 square of baker's chocolate.

To replace cocoa with carob, use equal amounts.

Sweeteners. As we have mentioned earlier, too much refined sugar in the diet has been linked to tooth decay, hypoglycemia, diabetes, allergies, hyperactivity, and other health-related problems. White sugar contains only empty calories, with no vitamins and minerals. Calories packed in fruits and vegetables are natural sugars, containing vitamins, minerals, fiber, and water, which cause a slow release of sugar in the blood stream.

All sweetners are not created equal. Raw sugar, brown sugar, honey, molasses, and maple syrup are concentrated forms of sweeteners high in calories and low in nutrients. (Molasses, honey, and maple syrup contain some iron, potassium, and calcium.)

Those who prefer honey should look for a locally produced honey—one that is labeled raw, unpasteurized, or unfiltered. Clover and tupelo honey are less likely to produce a "honey" taste. Dark bakery honey contains more minerals.

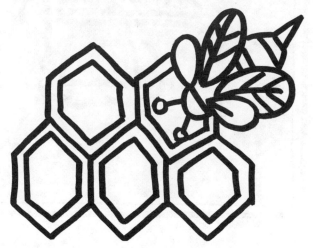

What about some healthier trade-offs?
Here are some ideas.

Replace white refined sugar with maple syrup, barley malt, sorghum or unsulfured molasses in the same proportions. Replace white sugar with honey according to this formula: For 1 cup sugar, use ½ cup honey and decrease the liquid by ¼ cup. If there is no liquid to decrease, then increase the flour by ¼ cup. Decrease the oven temperature by 25 degrees when baking with honey because honey browns quickly.

Replace 1 cup brown sugar with ¾ cup date sugar. Or use ½ cup honey and ¼ cup date sugar.

Increase nutrients by replacing 1 tablespoon of sugar with 1 tablespoon of unsweetened fruit juice.

Reduce the sugar by 2–4 tablespoons and increase the vanilla or almond extract by 1 teaspoon and increase the sweet spices (nutmeg, ginger, cinnamon, cloves, and allspice) by ½ teaspoons.

When substituting fruit juices in baking recipes, add ¼–½ teaspoons baking soda per cup of juice.

MAKE HEALTHIER COOKIES!

It's not difficult to convert "empty calorie" cookies into nutritious ones. Compare these two recipes, the first is loaded with sugar and made with white flour; the second one is sweetened with molasses, banana, and carob chips.

CHOCO OATIES
(REGULAR RECIPE)

1 cup shortening
2 cups sugar
2 eggs, beaten
1 teaspoon vanilla extract
1½ cups all-purpose flour
½ teaspoon salt
1 teaspoon baking soda
2½ cups uncooked oats
¼ cup chocolate chips

Cream together the shortening and sugar. Add the eggs and vanilla. Combine the flour, salt, and soda. Add alternately to the sugar mixture with the oats. Stir in the chocolate chips. Drop by the teaspoon onto an oiled baking sheet. Bake for 10 minutes in a preheated 350° F. oven, until browned. Cool thoroughly.

MAKES 5 DOZEN COOKIES

CAROB OATIES
(CONVERTED RECIPE)

1 cup ripe mashed banana
⅔ cup oil
½ cup molasses
2 eggs, beaten
1 teaspoon vanilla extract
1½ cups sifted whole wheat flour
½ teaspoon salt
2½ cups rolled oats
¼ cup carob chips.

Place the bananas in a mixing bowl. Add the oil and molasses, stirring thoroughly. Add the eggs and vanilla and mix lightly. Combine the flour and salt and add to the banana mixture alternately with the oats. Stir in the carob chips. Drop by the teaspoon onto an oiled baking sheet. Flatten slightly with a fork. Bake for 10 minutes in a preheated 325° F. oven until lightly browned. Cool thoroughly.

MAKES 5 DOZEN COOKIES

COOKIES

FAVORITE SUGARLESS COOKIES

1   cup unbleached flour
1   teaspoon baking powder
⅛   teaspoon salt
½   cup butter or margarine, softened
1   cup finely chopped walnuts
1   cup unsweetened coconut
½   cup chopped dates
½   cup chopped raisins
2   eggs, beaten
2   teaspoons vanilla extract

Mix the flour, baking powder, and salt. Cut in the butter until the particles are the size of peas. Stir in the nuts, coconut, dates, raisins, eggs, and vanilla. Mix until well blended. Chill the dough for 1 hour (or overnight). Shape in 1-inch balls. Place ½ inch apart on a nonstick cookie sheet. Flatten with a fork dipped in flour. Bake in a preheated 350° F. oven for 15 minutes or until lightly browned. Watch them disappear. These cookies store well—if they last that long. They also freeze well.

MAKES 3 DOZEN COOKIES

CAROB CHIP COOKIES

1¼ cups whole wheat flour
¼   teaspoon salt
½   teaspoon baking soda
⅓   cup butter or oil
⅓   cup honey
1   egg, beaten
1   teaspoon vanilla extract
1   cup carob chips
1   cup chopped nuts

Sift the dry ingredients together. Cream the butter, honey, egg, and vanilla. Add the dry ingredients to the creamed mixture. Add the carob chips and nuts. Drop by teaspoon on an ungreased cookie sheet. Bake in a preheated 350° F. oven for 10–12 minutes. These cookies freeze and store well. Delicious.

MAKES 3 DOZEN COOKIES

TREE TOP NUGGETS

½ cup chopped dates
½ cup chopped raisins
1 cup boiling water
½ teaspoon salt
1 teaspoon vanilla extract
1 teaspoon lemon juice
1 cup chopped nuts
2 cups mashed bananas
4 cups rolled oats

Place the dates and raisins in boiling water in a saucepan and simmer for 15 minutes. Place the date and raisin mixture in a blender; add the salt, vanilla, lemon juice, and blend until smooth. Place in large bowl. Add the nuts, bananas, and rolled oats. Mix thoroughly. Drop by a teaspoon onto a nonstick cookie sheet and flatten with a fork. Bake in a preheated 325° F. oven for 30 minutes; then reduce the heat to 225° and bake 30 minutes longer, until lightly browned.

These cookies tend to soften so for a crispier texture, reheat in the oven.

MAKES 4 TO 5 DOZEN COOKIES

OATMEAL CRUNCH COOKIES

3 cups rolled oats
1 cup whole wheat flour
1 cup unsweetened apple juice
¼ teaspoon cinnamon
½ cup chopped raisins
½ cup chopped dates
½ teaspoon almond extract
1 cup warm water
1 banana, mashed
½ cup chopped nuts

Mix the oats, flour, and apple juice in a large bowl. Stir in the cinnamon, raisins, and dates. Mix the almond flavoring in warm water and add to flour mixture. Stir in the banana and nuts. Place in the refrigerator for 15 or 20 minutes to chill. Mix again and drop by teaspoon onto a nonstick cookie sheet. Bake for 20 minutes in a preheated 350° F. oven.

MAKES 3 TO 4 DOZEN COOKIES

BANANA OATMEAL COOKIES

3 bananas
⅓ cup vegetable oil
2 cups rolled oats
1½ cups chopped dates
½ cup chopped walnuts
1 teaspoon vanilla extract
¼ teaspoon vegetable salt or salt
   substitute

In a large bowl, mash the bananas and add the remaining ingredients. Mix well. Drop by rounded tablespoons onto a nonstick cookie sheet. Bake 20–25 minutes in a preheated 350° F. oven. Remove to wire rack to cool. These cookies stay moist and freeze well.

MAKES 2 TO 3 DOZEN COOKIES

KID COOKIES

In hot, humid weather, serve homebaked cookies straight from the freezer. Don't defrost! They're refreshingly cool and super crisp.

YUM BALLS
(NO-BAKE COOKIES)

1   cup creamy peanut butter
2   cups shredded coconut
¼   cup chopped cashews or other nuts
1   tablespoon orange juice concentrate
½   cup chopped dates
½   cup sunflower seeds
¼   cup applesauce

Combine all the ingredients in a bowl. Mix well and roll into 1-inch balls. Place on a cookie sheet and refrigerate until firm. Watch them disappear! For an added treat at holiday time, place each ball in a candy-size paper liner.

MAKES 2 DOZEN COOKIES

GRANOLA BITES TO GO

1　cup whole wheat flour
1　cup unbleached flour
½　teaspoon baking powder
½　teaspoon cinnamon
1　teaspoon allspice
2　eggs
2　tablespoons safflower oil
1　cup unsweetened applesauce
2　tablespoons orange juice concentrate
2　cups unsweetened granola
¼　cup mixed dried fruit, diced (optional)

Stir the flours, baking powder, and spices together in a bowl. Beat the eggs and add the oil, applesauce, and juice concentrate. Combine with the flour mixture. Stir in the granola and dried fruit. Drop by teaspoonfuls onto a non-stick cookie sheet. Bake 10–20 minutes in a preheated 350° F. oven until the cookies are browned evenly and the tops spring back when pressed lightly. These cookies freeze well.

MAKES 4 DOZEN COOKIES

POWER-PACKED (NO-BAKE) COOKIES

These cookies are packed full of good nutrition. A handful of these cookies with milk or cheese and some fresh fruit makes a complete on-the-go meal.

½　cup peanut butter
¾　cup sunflower seeds
½　cup raisins or dates
¼　cup powdered milk
4　tablespoons date sugar
Shredded coconut or nut meal

Mix all ingredients together except the coconut or nut meal. Shape into balls the size of walnuts; then roll in the shredded coconut or nut meal until completely covered. Place in the freezer until firm. Pack in plastic bags or plastic wrap.

MAKES 18 COOKIES

ISLAND BARS

¾ cup whole wheat flour
¾ cup unbleached flour
1½ cups rolled oats
¾ cup butter
½ cup shredded coconut
½ cup chopped nuts

4 cups chopped dates
2 cups crushed pineapple in natural
   juice
¾ cup water
1 teaspoon vanilla extract

Mix together the flours, oats, butter, coconut, and nuts until you have a crumb mixture. Press half of it into a 9-inch by 12-inch pan and bake in a preheated 350° F. for 15 minutes.

While the cookie bakes, combine the dates, pineapple, water, and vanilla. Cook until thick and smooth. Spread on the baked crust. Sprinkle the remaining crumbs over the bars and pat down well. Bake at 350° F. for 30 minutes. Cut into bars when cooled. These travel very well.

MAKES 10 BARS

PEANUT BUTTER CAROB BROWNIES

12 ounces carob chips or nuggets,
   unsweetened
¾ cup peanut butter
2 cups rolled oats
1 cup granola

Combine the carob chips and peanut butter in the top of a double boiler. Cook over low heat, stirring constantly, until smooth. Remove from the heat and stir in oats and granola. Pour into a 8-inch by 9-inch nonstick pan. If desired, sprinkle chopped peanuts on top. Chill and cut into squares.

MAKES 2 DOZEN BROWNIES

POPCORN POINTERS

Too pooped to pop? Here are some quick additions for an old favorite.

★ Try popcorn mixed with nuts, dried fruit, toasted coconut or sesame sticks.

★ Serve popcorn with soup.

★ Sprinkle warm popcorn with grated Parmesan for taste teasers.

★ Add a spice—curry, tarragon, or basil—to heated oil and pour over popcorn.

★ Mix 4 cups of popcorn with 1 cup grated cheddar cheese. Place in low oven until the cheese melts.

★ Popcorn is not only a good munchie, but it also goes well as a mix-in or topping on soups and salads.

★ Watching your weight? 1 cup of *plain* popped popcorn has only 54 calories.

★ If you have a microwave, you can pop a bowl of popcorn (without using any oil or butter) in just 3 minutes.

CREAMY CAROB FUDGE

3 cups unsweetened carob chips
3 tablespoons milk
1 cup peanut butter
1 cup chopped walnuts

Combine the carob and milk in the top of a double boiler and cook over low heat until the carob is melted. Add the peanut butter and blend well. Remove from the heat and add walnuts. Pour into an 8-inch square nonstick pan. Allow to cool. Cut into squares.

14 SERVINGS

GOBLIN CRUNCHIES

1 large (no sugar added) carob candy bar
1 cup popped corn
1 cup chopped nuts

Melt the candy bar slowly in the top of a double boiler. Stir in the popcorn and nuts. Spoon into mini cupcake liners and place in refrigerator or freezer until firm.

Variation: Rice Krispies™, wheat cereal, puffed rice, or puffed wheat can be substituted for the popcorn.

6 SERVINGS

FRESH FRUIT

Fresh fruit is the all-natural sweet, ideal for packing. Fresh seasonal fruit or unsweetened frozen fruits are delicious eaten alone or combined with other fruits.

★ Pack colorful fruit wedges and tuck in cubes of cheese or mini cheese balls rolled in sesame seeds or poppy seeds.

★ Scoop out a cantaloupe boat and fill with strawberries, cubes of honeydew, watermelon, pineapple, or sliced bananas. Top with blueberries or dark purple grapes.

★ Pineapple wedges mixed with green grapes, orange slices, and red cherries, garnished with fresh mint and whipped cream or yogurt make a colorful and enticing treat.

★ For finicky eaters, try layering fruit ambrosia in a clear container. Combine cubes or balls of honeydew melon and cantaloupe, wedges of red and green apples, pineapple, peaches, and plums, orange segments, seedless grapes, and blueberries, strawberries, or raspberries. Really, any combination will do. Send along a topping of plain yogurt mixed with applesauce and sprinkle on granola, nuts, or coconut.

★ Make a Fruit and Granola Parfait: Place in a wide-mouth thermos layers of sliced strawberries, green grapes, and unsweeted granola. Pack in a separate container ¼ cup vanilla yogurt to spoon over the fruit parfait.

★ Make Orange Cream Cheese to use as a cake or cookie frosting or for frosting slices of apples. Cream together ⅓ cup cream cheese and ⅓ cup orange juice concentrate. Add 1 teaspoon vanilla extract if desired.

★ Make Fruit Snow: Place chunks of your favorite fresh fruit in a blender with a small amount of unsweetened pineapple juice, and process until smooth. Pour into ice cube trays and partially freeze. Return to the blender and mix again. Refreeze until solid. Pack in a wide-mouth thermos.

HOW TO CUT AND SERVE FRESH PINEAPPLE

Lay pineapple on its side. Using a heavy, sharp knife, cut in half lengthwise beginning at the base and cutting through the leaves at the top.

Place cut-sides down and cut lengthwise once again, making four wedges.

Working with one wedge at a time, cut away the hard center core.

Work the knife under one side, then the other to free the pineapple from shell. Do not remove the shell.

To serve, leaving shell intact, cut the pineapple in half lengthwise. Then cut crosswise into 1-inch chunks. Repeat with remaining three wedges.

To serve pineapple chunks, stick toothpicks into several pieces or eat with a spoon.

FRUIT LEATHERS

Fruit leathers are delicious dried fruit snacks. Store the leathers in airtight containers.

1 **(20-ounce) can crushed pineapple in natural juices**
¼ **cup shredded coconut**

Preheat the oven to 150° F. Pour the pineapple into a wire strainer and drain for 10 minutes, pressing out as much juice as possible (save for a fruit cup). Place the pineapple in the blender or food processor and process until smooth, stirring frequently with a rubber spatula. Stir in the coconut.

Line 2 large cookie sheets with plastic wrap. Spoon the pineapple mixture into 6 mounds about 3 inches apart on each cookie sheet. With a spatula, spread each mound to a 5–6-inch circle. Place in the 150° F. oven for 6 or 7 hours. If you have a food dehydrator, place the fruit mixture on plastic wrap on wire racks and turn on low heat overnight. When dry, peel off circles from plastic and roll into cone shapes. Wrap individually in plastic wrap.

MAKES 9 TO 10 ROLLS

Peach Variation: Substitute 1 (29-ounce) can of sliced peaches for pineapple; omit the coconut. Drain the peaches well; pat the slices dry with paper towels. Puree the slices in a blender or food processor; prepare the cookie sheets as above. You will need 1 extra small sheet. Spoon the puree into about 14 mounds; spread and dry as above.

Strawberry Variation: Substitute 1 (16-ounce) container of frozen strawberries, thawed and well drained, for the pineapple. Omit the coconut. Pat the berries dry with paper towels. Puree and pour into about 9 circles. Dry as above.

FINGER-LICKIN' STUFFED DATES

½   cup peanut butter
¾–1 cup non-fat dry milk
¼   cup mashed bananas or applesauce
1   (12-ounce) package dates

Combine the peanut butter, dry milk, and applesauce and mix well. Pit the dates and stuff with the mixture. Individually wrap in plastic and store in the refrigerator.

6 SERVINGS

BABOON BITES

Peel and cut 2 medium-ripe bananas into bite-size pieces. Dip each piece into a mixture of half milk and half pineapple juice. Drop the pieces into a bag of granola and shake until coated. Spear with a toothpick before packing.

2 SERVINGS

MIXED-UP MUNCHIES

This mixture is yours to create. Proportions don't really matter. Dried fruit, seeds, and nuts are the base. So mix whatever you like. Here's a recipe to begin with.

½ **cup raisins**
½ **cup hulled, unsalted pumpkin seeds**
1 **cup roasted soy beans**
½ **cup unsalted and chopped cashews, peanuts, or walnuts**
½ **cup shredded coconut**

Mix and refrigerate in an airtight container. Pack in small containers or plastic sandwich bags for individual servings. Other possible ingredients include: sunflower seeds, toasted soy nuts, date chunks, dried pineapple, dried banana or apple chips, sesame sticks, coconut chunks, and carob chips.

MAKES ABOUT 1 POUND

FROZEN AT-HOME TREATS

BANANA DELIGHT

Remove the skin from 1 ripe, medium-size banana. Wrap the banana in foil or freezer wrap and secure the ends tightly. Place in the freezer until frozen. Remove and pack in an insulated container. This is an excellent way to use up too-ripe bananas (or save dollars and purchase "ripe" bananas). Freeze up a batch ahead and enjoy the "ice cream" taste.

Variation: Dip the banana in plain yogurt and roll in one of the following before freezing: wheat germ, crushed fruit, sesame seeds (for calcium), finely ground toasted soy nuts, or bran.

Or, roll the banana in shredded coconut, ground nuts, granola, chopped dates, or peanut butter. Freeze.

1 SERVING

FROZEN CAROB BANANAS

4   ounces carob chips or nuggets
2   small bananas, ripe but firm
Ground nuts

Place the carob in the top of a double boiler over low heat until melted, stirring occasionally. Allow to cool. Cut the bananas in half crosswise and insert an ice cream stick about 1 inch into the cut end. Dip the bananas into the lukewarm carob, twirling to coat completely. Roll in ground nuts or crushed seeds. Keep frozen.

MAKES 4

STRAWBERRY YOGURT POPSICLES

1 (10-ounce) package frozen
　　　strawberries, thawed
½ tablespoon unflavored gelatin
8 ounces plain yogurt
6 paper cups, 3-ounce size
6 wooden sticks

Drain the strawberries and reserve the liquid. Place the liquid in a saucepan and sprinkle the gelatin on top. Cook over low heat, stirring constantly until the gelatin dissolves.

Mix the strawberries, yogurt, and gelatin in a blender or food processor until smooth. Pour into the cups. Cover the cups with foil. Insert a stick into each popsicle through a slit in foil over each cup. Freeze until firm. Peel off the cup when ready to eat.

MAKES 6

ORANGE YOGURT SNOW

8 ounces plain yogurt
1½ cups frozen orange juice concentrate
1½ teaspoons vanilla extract

Combine all ingredients in a blender and process until smooth. Pour into 4-ounce cups and place in the freezer until firm. (When partially frozen, you can insert popsicle sticks, if you wish; return to freezer until firm.)

4 SERVINGS

FAT-FREE SHERBET

1 cup buttermilk
½ cup pureed strawberries
½ teaspoon vanilla extract
Lemon juice to taste

Blend all ingredients and freeze in ice trays. Serve as cubes and garnish with a whole strawberry and fresh mint.

2 SERVINGS

SHAKE-UP POPS

½ cup cottage cheese
½ cup chopped fresh peaches
¼ cup non-fat dry milk
⅓ cup frozen orange juice concentrate

Place all the ingredients in a blender or food processor and process until creamy. Pour into 4-ounce paper cups and partially freeze. Insert a popsicle stick and freeze until firm.

3 SERVINGS

FRUIT POPS

Here's a way to use fruit that's either hung around the house too long or is on special sale at the fruit stand:

Use overripe bananas, peaches, plums, or nectarines (alone or in combination). Skin and pit the fruit, place the pulp in a blender, and blend to a puree consistency. Then pour into popsicle forms (available at houseware stores or supermarkets), or 3-ounce paper cups and place in freezer.

Variation: Pour fruit juice (grape, pineapple, orange, or whatever you like) into popsicle forms, ice trays, or paper cups and freeze.

PUDDINGS, SUNDAES, AND OTHER CREAMY TREATS

YOGURT SUNDAE

Use plain or vanilla-flavored yogurt and serve yourself toppings of peanut butter, nuts, carob chips, pineapple, strawberries, dried banana chips, honey or maple syrup. Kids love this treat, especially at a birthday party, but it works well to send some toppings along with a cup of yogurt for a school snack, too.

LEMON FROSTY

1   scoop ice cream
1   cup lemonade, chilled
Lemon slices
Sprigs of fresh mint

Place the ice cream in chilled thermos. Fill with cold lemonade. Place thinly sliced lemon floaters on top. Garnish with mint. When the ice cream melts, this still tastes delicious.

Variations: For Strawberry Frosty, use ¾ cup fresh strawberries, 1 scoop strawberry ice cream, and 1 cup skim milk. For Peach Frosty, use ¾ cup sliced fresh peaches, 1 scoop peach ice cream, and ½ cup skim milk.

1 SERVING

CAROB YOGURT

1 (4-ounce) unsweetened carob bar
8 ounces plain yogurt

Chop or grate the carob bar into the yogurt. Spoon into 4-ounce containers, cover, and chill or freeze. Remove from freezer or refrigerator and pack in wide-mouth thermos.

2 SERVINGS

FRUIT GELATIN DESSERT

For a basic recipe using plain gelatin and fruit, minus all the food coloring and sugary sweetening, combine 1 tablespoon unflavored gelatin with 2 cups warm unsweetened fruit juice. Stir until the gelatin is completely dissolved. Place in the refrigerator until slightly chilled. Remove from refrigerator and fold in 1 cup drained fruit. Pour into individual containers and store in the refrigerator until firm.

FROZEN STRAWBERRY YOGURT

Mix ½ cup plain, low-fat yogurt with ¼ cup chopped unsweetened frozen strawberries. Place in airtight container and freeze. This frozen dessert helps keep other lunchbox packables cold.

1 SERVING

FRUITY RICE PUDDING

2   cups water
1   cup uncooked brown rice
1   cup Almond Milk (page 148)
¼   cup unsweetened coconut
½   cup chopped raisins
¼   cup chopped dates
1½ cups unsweetened pineapple sections
2   bananas, sliced

Bring the water to a boil. Add the rice, cover, and bring to a boil. Reduce the heat and simmer for 1 hour, until the liquid is absorbed. Stir in the Almond Milk. Allow to cool slightly. Add the remaining ingredients and mix lightly. Spoon into wide-mouth thermos to serve warm.

Variation: For fresh berry pudding, replace ½ cup of Almond Milk with ½ cup yogurt. Stir in 1 cup fresh, washed and drained, berries (blueberries, strawberries, or raspberries) and ½ teaspoon almond extract. Omit the raisins and pineapple.

6 SERVINGS

GINGER CAKE WITH PINEAPPLE GINGER SAUCE

1	cup plus 1 tablespoon flour
⅔	cup non-fat dry milk
1	teaspoon cinnamon
¾	teaspoon ginger
1	teaspoon baking powder
½	teaspoon baking soda
1	egg, lightly beaten
1	teaspoon vanilla extract
1⅓	cups apple juice concentrate
⅓	cup pineapple juice concentrate
¼	cup apple juice concentrate
1	1-inch slice fresh ginger, peeled
1	teaspoon arrowroot or cornstarch
¼	cup water

Combine the flour, dry milk, cinnamon, ground ginger, baking powder, and baking soda, and mix well.

Combine the egg with the vanilla. Stir into the dry mixture with the 1⅓ cups apple juice concentrate. Mix lightly but well.

Pour into 2 greased and floured 8-inch round cake pans. Bake in a preheated oven at 350° F. for 20 minutes.

While the cake bakes, combine the pineapple juice concentrate, the ¼ cup apple juice concentrate, and the fresh ginger in the top of a double boiler. Heat until simmering. Combine the arrowroot or cornstarch with the water. Stir to dissolve any lumps. Stir into the juice mixture. Heat, stirring, until thick. Remove from the heat. Remove the ginger. Chill.

When the cake has cooled, pour a third of the sauce on top of the bottom cake layer. Top with the other layer. When ready to serve, pour more sauce over the top layer. Pass around the remaining sauce. If packing the cake, wrap the cake in plastic wrap, and pour the sauce into a separate container.

12 SERVINGS

ABOUT THE AUTHOR

As former Director of Food and Nutrition Programs for Fulton County Schools in Atlanta, Georgia, Sara Sloan spent 31 years teaching and feeding students nutritiously. Sara originated the nationally acclaimed and award-wining *Nutra Program*, as well as the successful *Karry Out* and *Trim A Pound* programs. Within 5 years she increased student lunch participation in the Fulton County schools from 61 percent to 87 percent.

Sara holds a Master of Education degree from the University of Georgia, appears on national television and has had her own weekly television program on nutrition, health, and family meals. Her articles have been featured in *Redbook, Ladies Home Journal*, and *Prevention* magazines as well as others. Her many professional awards and honors include the *Nutrition Committee, International Reading Association; Honorary Fellow, International Academy of Preventive Medicine; Rachel Carson Memorial Award, National Nutritional Foods Association; Tooth Fairy Society of America Award.*

Sara Sloan is currently the national director of the *Nutra Program*, publishes the monthly newsletter, *Nutritioning Parents*, conducts nutrition seminars, and has authored five other books: *Children Cook Naturally, Nutrional Parenting, From Classroom to Cafeteria, Guide for Nutra Lunches and Natural Foods*, and *Yuk to Yum Snacks.*

INDEX